Fading Away

A Multi-Generational Family's Portrait of Alzheimer's Legacy

Evelyn Bell Bruce

Fading Away

A Multi-Generational Family's Portrait of Alzheimer's Legacy

Evelyn Bell Bruce

PUBLISHED BY:
BRENTWOOD CHRISTIAN PRESS
4000 BEALLWOOD AVENUE
COLUMBUS, GEORGIA 31904

Dedication

Mother and Daddy, We miss you so much.

My husband, for still loving and inspiring me, unconditionally; after all these years.

David and Charlie, Jr. for being the greatest sons a mother could ask for. I love you both.

My siblings, for love, encouragement, and your prayers.

My friends and family, who know me so well and still love me.

My Spiritual father, for teaching me to walk in my "Prophetic Destiny."

Most all, to my Lord and Savior Jesus Christ, for paying the price for me a long time ago.

Preface

There are many melodies played in our lives. Some are unchained, restrained, refined, tapping, a soft step, and at times prancing lively. Some are so sweet. The taste lingers like nectar on our palette.

The mind, it's grand central station of reasoning, a gathering place for the psyche. This mental arena boasts a myriad of thoughts, actions, deeds, and characteristics, both endowed and acquired. When in the course of our lives this vast holding cell begins to leak, shrink, and erode; the beautiful and clear melody begins to fade ... fade ... fade away ... slowly the soundness, the beat, becomes a faint, pale and weak touch. All of the memories, all of the fears, assemble no more ...

Contents

INTRODUCTION

Our Heritage - Our Destinies

"One generation passeth away, and another generation cometh; but the earth abideth forever". (Ecclesiastes 1:4) kjv

There are many things in our lives that define our eminence, our reputation, or benevolence based merely on our ancestral history. More importantly, our beginnings, lineage, [bloodline] or our heritage; and the legacy that follows. What is passed on to us will no doubt help to influence what we become. Our attitudes and precepts, our ambitions or, as some would put it our environmental state of mind. Are we a people willing to work and strive to be the best? Or are we the ones who are content to accept whatever propensities others define for us.

We are given the option of success, failure, or obscurity, that is our choice. It is the physical stratus of which many of us live out our lives. Many rely strictly on the intellectual, financial, and persona to sustain a "fully accomplished life." When, however, another nimbus gathers and precipitates a change in our ability to function in the same order, we may find ourselves in another stratosphere. In a state of inability to chart our own course. Where do we go? Who do we turn to? Have we laid up any treasures to draw from or have we spent our time concentrating on visuals rather than visions? Sight rather than foresight? Do we have a relationship with God? Are we able to withstand what may befall us?

"Lay not up for yourselves treasures upon earth, where moth and rust doth corrupt, and where thieves break through and steal. Matthew 6:19 kjv.

6

Our spiritual investment will be the one thing that will have to sustain our very existence. As time goes by, all physical, spiritual, or emotional resources, (something all the money in the world can never buy) that we have stored will have to come into play.

We are taught early on to prepare the generation that is our off spring to follow our path, as well as the one established before us. We take what is taught to us and teach to them. We pass on as much of an inheritance as possible to insure that there is a rapid replenishing for each generation. This is done early in our lives for a reason. Once we reach a certain age, we may or may not retain the ability to chart these courses. It is then our lives becomes subject not only to our heavenly father, as it had been all along, but to the ones assigned here on earth as the "custodial management over you staff". When this happens all the melodies, dramas, and events of our lives start to stage a resurgence and all that we can sometimes do is watch from the sideline, and what a sight we see.

We may even lose track of what is presently required of us because of the present memory lapses. As time goes by, it will become apparent to some of the people close to us what is happening, and to others, we may be totally misunderstood, misjudged, and mistreated. All of the latter defines us as victims.

For us to be able to look through the eyes of someone suffering such a fate, hopefully will enlighten, and heighten our understanding of the condition known as Alzheimer. Our faith in God, realizing we are not forsaken is what will sustain us. The portraying of the characters in this book serves only to illustrate the condition in a layman's term. In understanding God's ability to sustain us even in the face of this disorder, the term victim becomes victor.

Weeds Among The Tulips

We spend much time and resources in our lives in the pursuit of personal definition. God defines us as having been created in His image, however; in the course of many of our

7

lives we have allowed our images to be redefined in many other aspects. We can change or make adjustments to the outside, the part that can be seen by all eyes, and we can make a loud or soft sound transmit from the vocal cords.

The one thing that cannot be discerned by natural eyes and ears, are the thoughts and deeds of the heart and mind. For a person having the condition of Alzheimer or Dementia, these are vivid descriptions. In spite of the condition, if there is enough love and care employed upon these loved ones, there is peace and there is a tranquility.

CHAPTER 1

From A Blossom, A Bloom

Irma Forest Dobbson, had always sat on the soft cushioned bench by her kitchen window each morning while having breakfast and reading her devotional passages. For years she and her late husband Roy had made this their daily ritual, it was a time of day that they seemed to enjoy most, as Roy would put it "before God gets too busy." She had always loved that particular spot because she could look out at her flower garden that had for years been her pride and joy. Now it seemed the weeds had taken over and were flourishing in her tulip bed faster than she could keep up with them. Irma was also an avid reader and loved crossword puzzles and TV game shows. But this morning, for some reason, she kept peering through the crisp yellow curtains.

She kept trying to remember if she had pulled the weeds yesterday or was she supposed to do that today? Actually it had been months. The large bed right under the window that had once displayed a color wheel of beautiful tulips, now asphyxiated by the overgrown weeds and wild flowering.

In the past, Irma found solace pulling weeds and clipping wayward growing branches in her vast flower garden. She would describe this time as "Down here on my knees and visiting with the Good Lord, it doesn't get any better than this." She'd dig, transplant, and prune to her heart's desire. "Who on earth moved my tools, and my rake? And my sun hat! I do wish people would leave my things alone!" "Someone, I know it must have been Mamie! I just bet she was the one who came over and took it!" Mamie was one of her next door neighbors. They looked after her but never removed anything from her yard or the shed out back. "I just don't know why people take my things." Irma mused.

She looked over at the untidy stack of newspapers, magazines, and an unfinished puzzle ... I thought I finished that puzzle, I know I did!" She mumbled to herself."

She thought of calling her daughter, Jenni, hoping she'd tell her where everything was hidden, but she didn't really like bothering her and she definitely didn't want Jenni trying again to force her to move out of her home and in with her; which would have been the best thing for Irma now that they both were widowed and Irma had becomes so forgetful. She really should not have been left to her own devices, and she was indeed exhibiting some very strange behavioral traits. Jenni was finding frozen uncooked food in the cupboards, cooked food left out on counters, and detergent and other dry staples in the refrigerator.

Jenni was becoming more and more frustrated with her mother. She loved her mother so much but all of the love in the world was not going to eliminate what she needed to do.

There were telephone listings of telemarketers having called and forced purchases on Irma, and in one case, she had given her credit card to one of them and they had run up thousands of dollars in bogus charges, for which she knew nothing about. Fortunately Jenni was able to legally reverse all charges to the company. She was able to do so because she had a legal power of attorney to act on her mother's behalf. Later Jenni would discover the necessity of other legal documentation.

Jennifer Marie Dobbson Cason, a widow, nicknamed Jenni for short, was Irma's only child. She had lost her husband unexpectedly a year ago.

"Maybe *I'll just wait a while! It'll come to me where I left them. I just don't know why people come in here hiding my things around! I know I put my sun hat over there just this morning and now it's gone too!*" ... She smelled smoke. "*Something's burning! What is that? Oh my gracious goodness! I must have left that dishtowel too close to the kettle!*" running to put out the fire, tossing the towel into the dishwater in the sink, and nearly falling over a large basket of clothes that have been in the same spot for about a week. *"What's wrong with me? I keep forgetting things!"* She thought about Roy and wished he was still there with her, life was so much easier when Roy was there to love and care for her, she thought.

The sound of the clock striking on the hour startled Irma, suddenly reminding her of her daily medication which she usually forgot to take after breakfast each morning. *"Oh, my goodness! I must remember my pills, Jenni says I must remember to take them at nine o'clock every morning! It's time to take them! One of these, one of these, and that black one. Oh my! I don't have another black one, I have to let Jenni know so that she can call the doctor."* She swallowed her pills washing them down with water and went back to her reading.

Trying to stay focused on anything, was a real challenge to Irma these days. As she sat there her mind started to wander back to her younger years. She could remember her siblings, her parents, and other childhood friends, but recalling even the simplest current details, at times, seemed more than she could cope with. Some days were more difficult than others. She felt herself slipping away, she was frightened at the very thought of losing control of her life, she prayed that whatever was happening to her was just a passing phase - but it wasn't.

It was quite amazing that a woman who just a few years before had been so productive and outgoing was losing control over everything around her, or so it seemed and sadly, she could not really comprehend all that was happening to her. People would whisper about her, but they never dared speak about it. It is sad that society does not confront issues of this type. It is as if the big pink elephant is sitting right in the living room on the couch, where everyone walks in, see it, but no one acknowledges its presence. Alzheimer disease is that elephant.

"Though I speak with the tongues of men and of angels, and have not charity, [love] I am become as sounding brass or a tinkling cymbal." (1 Corinthians 13:1) kjv

11

Irma spent years of her life in public service, in social work, a homemaker, and community activist. After retirement, she devoted a great deal of her time assisting people, especially the elderly, whom she really favored. On weekdays, she would deliver meals to the shut-in always taking the route near her home since she knew most of the older people who lived alone. She didn't just drop the food off but would go inside to check to make sure they were all right before leaving. Many times her van driver would become impatient because of her benevolence toward these people, but nothing stopped her from caring. Even as a younger woman with a small child, she recalled some of the people whose paths she had crossed. She loved everyone and this was her way of showing it, through her caring for those around her.

Helps - An Important Ministry In Life

"And God hath set some in the church, first apostles, secondarily prophets, thirdly, teachers, after that miracles, then gifts of healings, helps, governments, diversities of tongues". (1 Corinthians 12:28) kjv

Irma had a tendency these days to have flashbacks of her past years. These were usually very pleasant ones and she would some times even recall the names of some of the people she had cared for so lovingly. She thought of Mrs. Minnie Faison, one of the oldest members in her church and how when she made her rounds, Mrs. Faison would always ask her to come on in and sit down for a minute and read her mail to her, check her air cooler, go down to the corner A&P and cash her pension check, and bring her back some graham crackers, CC snuff, and a few bananas.*" And don't forget to give little Janie (meaning Jenni) a nickel so she can buy her something!"*Mrs Faison loved Jenni, even if she never got the name right.

Few people ever knew that Irma did this, she was not one to disclose her service or contributions to others. The way she looked at this was if God approved - that was sufficient for her. That was one of the many qualities her husband, Roy loved about Irma. He would often brag that "If you can't get along with my Irma, then you've got a problem, buddy!"

Mrs. Faison was nearly blind but her hearing was perfect, she could tell you verbatim everything that went on in the upstairs apartment where a young couple lived. She sat on her porch from the early morning until late afternoon when the evening sun would be so hot she would have to go inside and sit in her parlor. Irma knew Mrs. Faison needed a safe place to keep her money so she would secure it for her in the big Bible on the top shelf of the big Chiffarobe in the back bedroom so only she and Mrs. Faison knew where it was. And it would be there whenever she came to go to the store for her.

Irma was the only person other than her granddaughter, Priscilla, that Mrs. Faison trusted; since Priscilla lived across town, had four small children, and no car, Irma made it a point to look after her welfare. Mrs. Faison rarely used lights because she got up and went to bed with the "chickens." She would put her nightgown on at five o'clock sharp, and be in bed by six each evening.

Beautiful Petals Falling From a Rose
... how the ends do curl ...

Irma had always exhibited great faith in God, even as a child, and that is what motivated her spirit of giving of her time and love to others. She loved Saturdays, it was her favorite day of the week, she called it her "free day". She would make a lunch for Jenni, who was quite young at the time, and the two of them would visit the sick and shut-in; and helping out wherever she was needed. It was such a joy for these older people to see a little girl as friendly and well-mannered as Jenni, and as long as they kept their false teeth in their mouth, she'd sit with them. Once the dentures came out, Jenni wanted no more to do with them because she was afraid she'd lose hers too. She just could not understand why their teeth kept jumping out of their mouths when they talked. This was one of life's greatest mysteries.

13

When someone in the neighborhood was ill or had a new baby, they would visit, and Jenni loved the chance to hold the baby for just a minute, the smell of the new baby was so sweet, she'd beg Irma to get them a baby, and she promised to help with the baby. Irma would just smile. Irma set good examples for Jenni at a very early age. She wanted her little girl to grow up unselfish and kind to others just as she had. It worked! Because by the time Jenni was eight, she was bringing every stray dog, cat, or child home for dinner. Her father would just shake his head and say to Irma: "Yes, she's your daughter alright!

Like Mom Like Daughter-
Out of a blossom, comes a bloom

The diseases of Alzheimer and Dementia are close in resemblance but different in characteristics. So many times the elderly are mis-diagnosed, misunderstood, and mistreated because of these debilitating diseases. There are no cookie cutter symptoms associated with Alzheimer or Dementia. Like the seasonal daylight saving's plan "spring forward - fall backward" theory, much is being done today to advance the treatment of Alzheimers but not enough information is being provided in the media.

In many cases family members are sometimes reluctant to present this problem to professionals or even to their peers for many reasons; denial, fear, or even their pride keeps them from confronting this condition. When we are able to look this condition squarely in the face and accept its existence, we will be able to assist in the fight to find a cure. A cure that starts working before the symptoms are evidenced.

The vaccine against polio was once feared, but due to information and widespread communications, we have just about eliminated the disease from our modern populace. It our prayer and hope that one day this terrible condition will suffer the same fate. In the meantime let us not lose sight of the fact that we have a source of strength from which we can draw, a spiritual strength. We are not forsaken and we are not alone.

CHAPTER 2

Pebbles of The Past

Irma managed to fold her laundry, shaking her head in disbelief that she had neglected to get it done before now, and turning to check all four burners on the stove again to make sure they were off. She frequently walked back as many as three times to the kitchen to "check things" simply because she could not remember if she already had. She didn't want a repeat of this morning. She was fighting hard to prove to Jenni that she was capable of living alone. Her mind still seemed bent on spinning webs. *"God help me I am losing my mind!"* She would anguish herself.

She had a terrible habit of turning the faucet on to test the water, and then leave it running for long periods of time. Jenni was always trying to figure why the water bill was so high with only one person living in the house. It would be just a matter of time "before the place was totally flooded." She fumed.

Irma had been widowed for three years, having been thrust suddenly into independence since Roy had died of a massive stroke one night after returning from a baseball game. The doctors said he had shown symptoms before but he chose to ignore his high blood pressure, he didn't like taking medicine, and his diet and exercise programs never got off the ground. He refused to listen to their advice preferring, *"The good life,"* as he would put it. Irma always wished that he wouldn't, but there seemed to be no stopping him. That is what made Roy happy and his happiness meant everything to her.

Irma was the love of his life, he would be at her beck and call to help with the shopping, banking, or whatever. He devoted

15

all of his retired years to her. She had no concerns as to what was in their checking, savings, or investment accounts until his death. She had never taken an interest in that sort of thing. When Roy would try to get her to look into these matters, she would just dismiss it: "I trust you to take care of everything for us, I don't see why I should concern myself with worrying about things like that!" She managed whatever Roy provided very well. Roy would just shake his head and mumble under his breath *"I don't know what she'll do without me ... maybe Jenni will take over."*

He knew that Jenni had responsibilities for her own family, catering to the domineering man she'd married, she had put aside her career to stay at home to raise Caron and Jimmy, so Roy's death was the most traumatic thing that had ever happened in Irma's seemingly perfect life.

Love and happiness, Too Soon Gone

Roy's death was to Irma like a jack-hammer pounding on cement, literally breaking it all apart. Unfortunately, she suffered a near nervous breakdown, and had to be hospitalized for several days, and she was never the same again. Irma would earnestly pray to God to take her out of this world because she did not know how to be here without the man she had been so deeply in love with for most of her life. From the Sunday morning that she sat on the back bench in that country church, she knew they were destined to be together forever. *"Why, Roy, why, why did you have to leave me here?"*

Jenni was Roy's *"little butterfly"*, the ideal daughter. She was an ideal wife to Jim, and the ideal mother (*a super mom*) to their two children. She had been taught balance early in life, so she was prepared to be the kind of woman, friend, and wife that Jim Cason desired.

Irma had always invested her time cultivating her daughter and teaching her right from wrong. She knew that if she instilled values in her at an early age, they would always be there. Irma was a virtuous, balanced young woman and she legislated Jenni to be no less. Even as a student Jenni was disciplined, even away from home in college which in itself boggled her roommates. She was the kind of girl who paid attention to every detail. A sense of pride was instilled in her early in life, when things were not nearly as complicated as they are now. Jenni provided well for her family spiritually and culturally. Her children were required to clean their rooms daily, use their time wisely and always finish what they started. Jimmy was a talented and gifted child who always came home with a gold star. Caron did well too, but she didn't always get a star, nor did it bother her if she didn't.

Sometimes their father would chide her about it and Jenni would come to her defense. She had a rule to never compare her children, but accepted them as each being unique in their own way. This was one woman whose husband should have had no trouble praising her in the gates of the community because she made it her life's occupation to be the best that she could be, thanks to a great mother like Irma.

She treated Jim like a king, and he treated her like "this was his castle and he was king". Jenni was so entranced in him, it seemed as if she was literally drunk with love and adoration for her husband. Jim loved her just as much, he was just more of an intimate person, and Jenni wanted the world and all of its neighbors to know about their love. Roy and Irma were not that impressed with their future son-in-law at first, but because Jenni loved him, and they loved Jenni, they conditionally accepted him. In their opinion Jim was too arrogant and self-centered, but also ambitious and successful and he did provide a very comfortable existence for his family.

The first time Jenni brought Jim home to meet her parents and have dinner, he spent most of the time talking about himself, his dreams, schemes, and plans; and seemed to talk down to Jenni and patronize Irma whenever they interjected anything in the conversation. Really *"amazing that a boy that young could have such conceited ways"*, Roy had thought, but Jenni didn't seem to mind, she thought the sun rose and set on Jim.

17

On April Fools day, a couple of months after Jim had come to dinner, Irma and Roy received a very frantic phone call from Jenni, she was so excited, *"Guess what Mom and Dad! Jim asked me to marry him. I said yes, and we are getting married next June! Dad, Jim wants to come and speak to you and Mom and ask for my hand this weekend, is that okay?"* "Well, I guess so baby, I uh, we will see you then".

The rest of that week was torture for Roy, he was not ready to relinquish his baby girl to any man just yet. He hadn't even met this boy's family yet, but they were coming to meet them soon too, since Jim's parents were just as surprised as Jenni's parents.

"How was he going to support her, did he have a job? Where was he going to put her? There was no way he was going to stand for this! But Irma was calm, she cried, she planned, she cooked and she put her hands on her hips and told Roy "if you do anything to spoil Jenni's weekend, you will be sleeping outside in the doghouse with Roady." Roady was Jenni's eighteen year old German shepherd. Roy had gotten her that dog as a pup when she was just about four years old. Roady was getting old and arthritic, and would soon have to be put down, but Jenni would not allow it until she'd finished college, "then I'll think about it".

Note: *A person having the genes for this disease might not exhibit any symptoms for years, and then suddenly a traumatic event occurs in their lives such as: the lost of a spouse, or a child. Other trauma could be an injury from falling, a series of small strokes, or some other intense situation. The loss of one's spouse is probably the most common trigger function to launch this disease into swift progression. The body looks the same. Their surroundings rarely change.* It is important to note that this not a medical analysis only an opinion of an experienced caregiver. Note: **Many victims suffer for years … in silence.**

CHAPTER 3

Jenni's Rainbow

That weekend turned out very well and it was the turning point in Roy and Jim's relationship. When Jim convinced them that he had already been offered a top paying position for a large aeronautics manufacturing company in that area, and he would be able to afford to build a home for them within six months, Roy was impressed, very impressed. He was also relieved, because he didn't want to have to answer to Irma.

Jenni and Jim's wedding was one of the most beautiful ever witnessed in that church, beautiful fresh flowers and tulle draping everywhere, and lots of candles. Their reception was a sit down dinner for two hundred people, a beautiful cake nearly five feet tall, and covered with beautiful white gum-paste and fondant flowers that matched the ones on the pews and on the long linen covered tables in the banquet hall. Jenni wore a beautiful antique white satin gown trimmed with mother of pearls and chantilly lace, designed by La Chere's of New York, an exclusive designer that her future sister-in-law introduced her to. Her veil was a floor length Alencon lace mantilla carried by the four year-old twin son and daughter of one of Jenni's childhood friends. Jim was so handsome in tall hat and tails. His best friend, Dexter Jordan Clayton, an Army Captain, a childhood pal, was his best man. It was the talk of the town. Irma and Roy beamed with tears, pride and praise at the sight of their little girl so beautiful, so happy, and so pure.

Shortly after they were married, Jim joined their church and became actively involved. He and Jenni, the Pastor, Reverend

Fred Sykes, and his wife Leah, a thirty-something couple with two small children, became very good friends. Eventually Jim started teaching Sunday School, was promoted to Superintendant, and Jenni worked with the youth groups. During the first two years of their marriage, Jenni taught high school then they decided to start a family. When their first grandchild *Caron Ashley Cason*, was born, Irma and Roy shed tears of joy, and that was the event that started Grand Pa Roy back to attending church a little more faithfully. He didn't want to miss anything that might pertain to his precious grandchild.

Jenni had planned to return to her teaching position, which she loved; as soon as Caron was old enough to be left with her grandma but Jim would not hear of it, so she stayed at home and two years later, Jimmy was born. Irma and Roy enjoyed visiting and doting over their grand children. Irma would make all kinds of goodies, and special gifts for them, read Bibles stories and teach them lots of games. They loved their grandparents, but as they grew up and began to get more involved in all of the activities they spent less time with them. Jenni would always insist they telephoned or wrote a nice note each time they received gifts or cards from them. They were well-mannered and intelligent children.

By this time, Jim had moved into a very well paid position in his company and Jenni was the perfect corporate wife. They were a model family in the eyes of their friends and colleagues. They knew all of the *right people*. It gave him a sort of one upmanship to be able to boast his children's scholastic and social attributes. Irma wondered where everyone was now? *"Why had everyone deserted her and taken all of her things, why had they left her like this?"*

She was still looking everywhere for those gardening tools *"Who on earth moved my gardening tools, and my sun hat! I do wish people would leave my things alone!"* *"Somebody ... must have been Mamie"*. Her neighbors looked after her but they never removed anything from her house. *"I know where I put them ... I just don't know why people bother my things. ... I thought I finished that puzzled, I know I did!" She thought out loud to herself, "perhaps if I call Jennie, she'd know where everything is ... no ... I won't bother Jennie she has enough on her mind now, with Jim gone ... Maybe if I try real hard I can remember. Lord, please help me to remember these things!"*

Jenni, her only child had lost her husband, Jim, a year ago, he had suffered a massive heart attack while playing tennis, after work one afternoon. They had just celebrated their twenty-second anniversary a month earlier. Their two children, Caron and Jimmy were away at school. Caron in her Junior year at Radcliff; and Jimmy a freshman, at a Theological University in Oklahoma. Jenni had been trying for months to convince Irma to sell that big house and move in with her so that she could keep a better watch over her. There had been a few calamities in the past months that warranted it. She had hope that being patient would help her mother to relent, but no so far. Jenni would eventually find herself in court having Irma declared incompetent to care for herself. That was something she did not look forward to. She knew that Irma would just die. Only God knew and understood how Jenni felt because she had not discussed these problems with anyone else. She was constantly bewildered - When we find ourselves "losing it" we grasp for invisible structures; the ones we used to take for granted.

Irma was becoming very confused and having a lot of trouble remembering the common things in her present day to day life. She seemed to have to concentrate so hard, to properly dress herself, sometimes remembering what a ringing phone meant, or the urge to go to the bathroom. Once she had awaken from a deep sleep to find, as she had put it, *"Someone poured water in my bed!"* She was sometimes dressing in several layers of clothes when she went out. On days when the temperatures soared, rather than turn on the air conditioner, she'd put on a sweater, or get completely undressed. There was no way to really predict this sudden behavior. Her conversations were basically a reliving of her past, her childhood, young married years, and Jenni's younger years. She had little trouble these days remembering those wonderful years gone by.

21

CHAPTER 4

Beautiful Petals Falling From The Rose

Remember now thy creator in the days of thy youth,
while the evil days come not, nor the years draw nigh,
when thou shalt say, I have no pleasure in them.
(Ecclesiastes 12:1) kjv

Growing up during the depression, in one of the big old drafty, five bedroom brownstones on Cauley Avenue, where she, her parents, Hilton and Ellien Forest, her grandmother, Pearlie Hodges, and three other siblings lived, Audrey, her older sister, two brothers, Earnest, three years her senior, and her younger brother, Robert James.

Their father worked in the newspaper printing plant, their mother, worked as a domestic. She cooked and cleaned for the rich up on Nob Hill Lane, and came home each day to do the same for her family. Irma remembered waking up to her mom's egg-biscuits and bacon, coffee perking, the sound of the old crank-armed wringer washing machine rocking and roaring in the next room, and the smell of Clorox. Her mother would wake them very early to insure that they ate a hearty breakfast and had clean starched and ironed clothes for school each day.

They walked together through the gray haze of tenant buildings, the eight blocks to Sullivan Street School. Ellien would have Audrey prepare the lunch bags, and Earnest was responsible for filling the coal buckets for the heaters each morning and evening.

Irma and Robert James, the two younger children, had two main chores. One was to clean out the contents of Grandma

Pearlie's "snuff-can" and refill with sand, (a chore which they both hated), and the other was to sweep the steps in the hallway and the front stoop outside which they didn't mind because this always gave them a chance to sneak around the corner and peek into "Sister Dora Lee Frye's Prayer Parlor" window and see who was in there getting their fortune told, or as the church folks called her the "Prayer Lady.' In reality, she was classified as a fortune teller. She always wore black from head to toe. And the only part of her face they had ever seen was her really large almond shaped eyes, that looked like spiders from all of the mascara. Her husband, a much older and very frailly looking man was rarely seen, it was said that he was a little off and had been in and out of mental hospitals so she had to care for him as well as do business with the public.

For fifty cents, Sister Dora would lay hands on you, gaze into her crystal ball, and declare an appropriate blessing on you instantly, afterwards she always served a pot of steaming hot sassafras root tea and cold spiced tea cakes to soothe the sorrows of the poor dejected soul who had so innocently brought her their hard earned money.

Their grandmother, Pearlie Hodges, had been known to give Sister Dora a coin or two, when she got her widow's pension check each month. Ellien would scold her about this but it didn't stop Pearlie. She would refer to it as her revelation. Irma and Robert James would perch themselves on the wide window ledge and listen to her as she wailed out those *prayers and predictions*, some good and some bad, they guessed she had to balance her act. Soon reality would hit them and they would remember to get back to the business at hand. They all had to pitch in and help out around the house.

Pearlie was somewhat disabled but could get around sufficiently to keep an eye on them until Ellien came home from work. She would mend or darn clothing during the day and since she was sort of forgetful Ellien never depended on her to cook the dinner or do laundry because there had been a few disasters since granny moved in and they all were attributed to her being

23

"old and senile" although she was only sixty-two at the time. It seemed to them that her "bread wasn't quite done." As some would whisper. She had been strange that way since her husband died. The children all loved her and obeyed her. They knew that if they did not they would pay a dear price with the strap when their dad came home from work. Hilton was not one to promise anything. He was a strict but a very loving disciplinarian who expected much from his offsprings. Every night after he blessed the table, and while they ate, he had a great new story to tell; one that he'd heard down at the printing plant and although he didn't have the chance to read the newspaper articles in detail, he would draw from the conversations he'd overheard coming from the news copy desks. Irma and Robert James couldn't wait for him to get home each night. Sometimes they used his stories as some of their current events homework

Hilton Forest, Irma's father, was no scholar, but reading and telling stories was his favorite pastime. After dishes and homework was done each evening, he would summon the four of them. They would sit on the big maroon velvet-covered divan in the parlor and listen while Hilton read scriptures or some other stories for a while or turned on the gramophone to listen to *The Gospel Four, Ella, and other greats;* and sometimes they would take turns playing the piano. Ellien had taught all of her children to play the piano just as Pearlie had taught her when she was a young girl. Hilton and Ellien wanted better for their children than they had. They wanted them to be educated and well versed, as he put it, *"Like those fancy folks down at that Newspaper."*

He implored them daily to *"study hard and get good grades, it'll benefit you later in life!"*

Irma now thought to herself," *where are those seventy-eight rpms that we always keep on the table next to the gramophone? Who in the world moved them?"* She remembered her parents loved to get dressed up in their nice clothes; Ellien in one of her pastel colored chiffon dresses, spike heels; and Hilton, all spiffy in his tailored grey pinstripe suit and his polished black and white wingtips, and his "applejack" hat. They would strut down to the *Starlight Lounge* on Jefferson Avenue and dance the night away. In those days, a man could take his wife out and not have to worry about safety in the streets.

Sundays they would gather the family and ride the trolley the five blocks to the North Thirtieth Street Missionary Baptist Church where Hilton was a senior deacon and trustee. Ellien played piano, and served on the Ladies Auxiliary Baptist Union Society.

One of the members, Sister Lucy Rollins, a rather big and strapping woman who wore a fur stole and a big broad felt hat always sat near them, to keep the children from talking and giggling. She had large wide feet and her high heeled shoes fit like a bowl around them. They would quietly tease behind her back calling her little nicknames. She would always get happy during the sermon and sometimes fling her big hat as she was shouting, causing it to go flying off in the distance. One time her wig had come off with the hat as she was jumping and shouting and she didn't realize it for about ten seconds, and when she did, that sort of took some of the power out of her shout. Even Reverend Lowell had trouble keeping his composure from the pulpit. Just looking at Sister Lucy trying to hide all of that nappy hair under that wig and still pretend to be happy at the same time was quite a site, and a little more than the children could handle, so a lot of snickering was going on behind her back. The ushers had to use their handkerchiefs to keep from laughing out loud as they sat her down. She lived alone in a small tenement apartment with very few conveniences, so she was always invited home with them for dinner after church. Ellien felt that no one should have to spend Sunday afternoon alone like that, so regardless of the fact that the children hated having to contend with Sister Lucy, she was their honored guest each week. They would come home and Hilton would bless the table adorned with hot cornbread, collard greens, fried chicken, potato salad, pound cake, and ice cold lemonade. After everyone had eaten, Ellien would wrap up a large portion for her to take home for a late night snack. Later some of their relatives would come over to visit and the rest of the day would be spent just laughing, talking, and torturing the kids about "how hard it was when they were children back in Eastward, Georgia." Uncle Walter and Uncle Jasper would chime in telling their "walking four miles barefoot in the snow to an unheated one room school house with no roof" stories.

As much as the kids heard these tales, they never really believed a word of it, especially the snow part. Their elders would tell them these things so as to instill in them a good attitude of hard work in order to succeed in life. Hilton had dropped out of school in the tenth grade, and Ellien had finished the eleventh grade, that was as far as they had to go to graduate in those days. It was important to him that he made *the best* provisions possible for his children to get a good sound education and have a better life.

Born of A Heritage
Out Of The Stormy Past, Treading,
Marking The Future

Ellien had been the pianist for the choir since she was just twelve years old. Her mother, Pearlie was the neighborhood piano and organ teacher and had taught Ellien to play when she was just "knee high to a duck" as the old folks who sat around listening to her would say. When she and Hilton got engaged everyone was concerned, especially after the rumors of their plans to relocate after their wedding, started circulating. They had been a part of that church all of their lives, it was difficult to even think of replacing them.

Reverend Moses, Ellien's father, had been the pastor of that church for at least thirty years, and his father had preceded him. It was difficult to even think of replacing any of them. They were considered pioneers of Mount Nebo Baptist Church. Moses' grandfather, had helped to build that church back in eighteen sixty-six, right after the emancipation was declared legal.

His mules carried the logs that were cut for that church. On Juneteenth day, they held their first service. It was the only church in town for about ten years. Later a Methodist preacher came to town and soon after there were two churches. By the turn of the century, there were four other denominations and many problems and arguments every week over who was right and who was not. From Missionary Baptist to AME Methodist to the Pentecostal, whom everyone regarded as those "Holy Rollies," all declared that their church and theirs only was the one that would get you in heaven.

No one wanted Ellien and Hilton to ever leave Eastward but a couple of months after they married, they left Georgia on the *Silver Star* Atlantic Coast Line, heading north to live with Hilton's first cousin Jake, who had left five years earlier, rather quickly. Seems there had been a problem with Jake keeping company with the wrong crowd.

Jake Lawyers was one of Ellien's cousins, on her father's side of the family. Jake had always managed to create problems for himself. Specifically, the problem with him keeping company with the wrong crowd, *and the wife of the biggest number runners in town.*

Jake rebelled against all that a church going Christian stood for or any thing else that was considered to him to be *"religious"* as he would so state. He was the topic of gossip for every household in the back quarters where they lived. Men hated him with a passion and women loved him with an even greater passion. Jake was extremely handsome, tall with jet black wavy hair and piercing grey eyes, his skin was as rich looking as *caramel.* He considered himself God's *"gift to womankind,"* while many others thought he was a little serpent.

Jake's family members were devout Christians, hard-working and honest, always willing to help others. Their father, Claude Lawyers, was a very soft spoken timid man, who had long ago given up any hopes of his sons amounting to anything. So he just kind of faded away into the background and allowed their pervasive behavior to thrive. Jake and his older brothers, Claude Jerome, Jr. whom everyone referred to as "June Bug", and Ephraim, nicknamed "Bingo", had on many occasions given them reasons for serious concern. Many nights his mother prayed aloud for hours that they would come home and clean up their act, but to no avail. Jake and "June Bug" rebelled against all that she or the church stood for. In fact, anything. "Bingo" was a little better as a son, but he had a lot of physical problems. He had tried out for the Bingo Long Traveling All-stars, but due to a leg injury, had been let go. He was never the same after that, so he just stayed near home and drank.

All of these things were a constant source of pain for their mother, Ninabelle, who was Moses' sister. They never realized their mother's importance until she dropped to the floor dead one night, while praying on the side of the bed. It appears she had suffered a heart attack but there were rumors that her size and weight had a lot to do with it. Ninabelle was four feet tall and weighed in excess of four hundred pounds. Whenever she walked you could hear her wheezing so loudly. She didn't have to knock because that sound alerted everyone within a block.

Ninabelle loved to cook and loved to eat even more. She usually ate an average sized fried chicken, big piles of mashed potatoes, four to five smothered pork chops, a whole mess of greens cooked in fatback, and a pan of buttered biscuits for dinner; and for dessert a big dish of fruit cobbler topped off with a dollop of fresh whipped cream and a big jar of iced tea. A body trying to digest that much food each meal in itself was more that her heart could handle. It took six men to get her enormous body into a cardboard foundation, pink satiny covered casket, that really was a wee bit too small. They almost made it, staggering in the intense heat to the grave site with her massive body, before it started to disintegrate at the bottom from all of that weight. It was such a sad sight. It took all that the Pallbearers could do to keep her in there until they could get it into the ground. That unfortunate incident still provided years of conversation.

"June Bug" was a big strapping, smooth, dark chocolate complexioned man with silky straight, processed hair and two big starred gold teeth in the front of his mouth. Every time he grinned they sort of sparkled. He was handsome but attracted a different class of women than Jake. There were a couple dozen children that he had fathered by four or five young women in the neighborhood, some he did not even know by their full name. Most of them seemed proud to have him as father of their beautiful children; even though he did very little to support them, or for that matter, even acknowledge them.

"Bingo" was tall and very, very skinny. But he could eat like two horses. He ate so much that as the old people used to say, it made him "po' to carry it". He was very handsome but since he had such low self-esteem, he was difficult to get along with, constantly in and out of bad relationships. He eventually straightened up his life and went on to become a minister.

One of Jake's admirers was of the Caucasian persuasion; and back in those days, that was a lynching offense. He had done some carpentry work for Mr. Mel Dayton, a white store owner and racketeer. Somehow, while he was supposed to be working, he managed to be distracted enough to be caught exiting this man's home in the middle of the afternoon. He found himself in a very pernicious situation. He had a big price to pay for this little bit of business. The police allowed the ego injured husband to retaliate.

In the segregated thirties and forties lynchings, cross-burnings, and other inhumanities were common practice. They tied Jake to a tree with cords, allowed Mel to beat Jake nearly to a pulp with a tire iron, brand him across his back, and then assuming he was dead, dumped him on the bed of a big supply truck leaving town.

Note: Juneteenth is normally observed in the south on June 17th or Jan. 1, depending on locale. Texas observes it on June 17th.

CHAPTER 5

Reasons For Serious Concerns

When Jake was found a week later, barely alive, nearly blinded from that beating, and freezing, still crouched on the bed of that truck which had been parked near the *Dundalk Shipyard*, he was hospitalized in the *Baltimore Colored Charity Infirmary* until he could recuperate enough to be transferred to the *Mercy Sisters Mission* down near the harbor where he worked in a fish market scaling fish, and shucking oysters and crabs until he had earned enough money to get a room in one of the boarding houses in the area, he immediately went back into business and flourished until he was arrested and imprisoned for racketeering.

A year later, Jake was released, and he went up to Newark, found a room, some work, some friends, and eventually saved enough to rent a real large house. He had a little help because he started running numbers again, this time on his own. Weekends, he would sell fish sandwiches, brew, and *Supercoolers* as a coverup for his numbers' business.

Hilton knew that Cousin Jake was a bit shady, yet he still loved his cousin and he knew that he and Ellien would have a place to live until they could find something better. By the time their first child, Audrey, was born, they had saved enough to get a three room flat on the west side of town.

Hidden Treasures Left Behind
The Importance of The Heritage

When Hilton's father's father, passed away from complications due to his mental state, (he became unable to swallow foods and eventually died of malnutrition), he and his brothers went back to Eastward to bury him. Rufus Forest, (everyone called him *Mr. Rufus*) was a very enterprising man, a real entrepreneur in the *Homemade Beverage* business and didn't believe in banks at all. So all of his life, he stashed money away in cans and jars. Although Hilton's mother had been a church going woman, Mr. Rufus never took church very serious, he went along just enough to keep her from fussing. Mr. Rufus had one of the largest, most sophisticated, and well hidden moonshine stills in the county. The police did not bother him too much because they consumed as much as they desired at any time of the day or night.

They would drive their *Black Mariah* deep into the woods and load it up with gallons of moonshine. Mr. Rufus also paid them off faithfully, and never gave his own customers one sip of that moonshine on credit. Even though he could not read or write, he kept track of every penny he earned, highly regarded as the stingiest man alive, counted them every night before he went to bed.

He was careful not to let on that he had this money, because in those days of such open and widespread Klan activity, it was dangerous for a colored man to possess large sums of money so that is why Mr. Rufus had secretly buried it. Only his daughter, Edwina, knew exactly where it was buried. Fortunately, before he lost his ability to communicate sensibly he had given her a diagram that he kept hidden under his mattress. He had instructed her to give it to the boys and they were to wait until dark each night before starting to dig. It was just too dangerous during the day.

Fortunately, it was winter time and there were no snakes to contend with, as would have been the case in the summer. Right after the funeral, they gathered their holediggers, shovels, and a big wheel barrel to get the job done. They dug for two nights in a row, only stopping every now and then for some chicory and a little snack that Edwina had prepared for them. They figured he had been canning money for at least thirty to forty years, He had customers who came from as far away as Virginia, and they all had to pay cash.

They recalled an incident once when a young Carolina man had tried to get away without paying, and had pulled a knife on Mr. Rufus. Unfortunately, he underestimated Rufus's strength. He was overpowered, beaten up and taken away by the local police and his body was found in a shallow creek a few days later. The rumor was, he tried to get away.

Determined to find every container, they did. There was over *Thirty-five thousand dollars* recovered from those rusty old containers. They were out done, not to mention scared. If the police or anybody for that matter got wind of this, they would have been killed and the money taken away. There was a hard and fast rule back then about blacks getting too uppity and having too much, especially land and money. Hilton, Walter, Jasper, and Edwina divided that money between them. Since their mother had passed away already, they had control of everything that was left. Edwina had nursed their mother faithfully after she became so senile and weak, that she could no longer feed or dress herself. (They were not aware of Alzheimer in those days, but looking back, that is her probable cause of death.) They gave Edwina the house and everything in it, hurriedly pack their things, hopped a freight train going north to Raleigh, and then catching a train back up north.

Irma was remembering her parents more and more these days. She knew that they were gone but she still treasured a few vivid memories. Her mind wandered back to those days growing up in Newark.

CHAPTER 6

Where The Heart Is At Ease

When Hilton returned home from his trip to Eastward, He and Ellien decided to buy a home for their children. They had been living in a small, back street, second floor walk up that they found near the area where Hilton worked. It was walking distance and since Ellien was able to get the trolley to work right around the corner, it was convenient. Now he wanted to find a lot more space for his family to grow. There were two children now, and Ellien was close to giving birth to Irma. The place was becoming more cramped each day. Hilton knew he had to act fast.

Each Sunday after church, Hilton would walk up and down streets in their neighborhood, and other areas, looking and praying to find a home for his family. He could find nothing that was sufficient for his family and when he did find something, it was in the wrong area, or he was the wrong race. The Celtics in that area controlled the racial and ethnic demographics in those days. One day unexpectedly, his prayers were answered. A very well-to-do man at his job, approached him and asked a favor, he needed someone to help repair some damaged pipes in his home, and he knew Hilton was very good with welding tools. Hilton went to this man's home up on the "rich side of town" spent all day Saturday and most of Sunday, repairing and restoring this man's pipes. Afterwards, he would accept no money for the job. The man was so taken aback because of Hilton's generosity, he didn't know what to do or say. Not even realizing that Hilton was looking for a house to buy, he told Hilton about a brownstone that he had owned down in Newark over on the North side of town and that it was for sale. Hilton excitedly went home got Ellien and the kids, took the trolley to Cauley Street, and were they delighted. That big old house was clean, painted, and ready for moving in, and *the price was right!* It was what they had prayed for. It was a real blessing for them. Ellien suddenly felt a sharp pain. Time was of the essence now.

A month after Irma was born, they moved into the brownstone, *Cauley Browns* as this section of town was called then. Some of the people living in this area were well to do and this is where Hilton wanted Irma and her siblings to grow up. He wanted to make sure they were proud and not beholding to anyone. Ellien had quit working for a while. Even though they were now in the middle of the depression years, and Hilton having used most of his cut of the money from Mr. Rufus's backyard bank to just about completely pay for that house, they were not suffering. Hilton made enough money to support the family. Ellien even had a little money each week to purchase pricillas for her front windows and chenille spreads for the beds.

Ellien's mother, Pearlie, had come to live with them after her father, Moses passed away. The two of them would sew, and quilt in their spare time, so they always had plenty of extra bed covers for company. Irma and Audrey shared a room, and her two brothers shared a room. Irma was a very precocious child when it came to mischief among her siblings but she dared not touch anything on Audrey's dressing table that she had fashioned from two orange crates covered with muslin and lace sewn around the bottom edges. Audrey would tell her in no uncertain terms that she was never to bother her things. While Audrey would be out on a date, Irma would use her hairbrush, make-up, and try on her new high heel shoes, her lacy slips and skirts, careful to place them precisely where they had been before.

She remembers waking up to loud voices late one night, someone yelling, and people crying, she could hear sobs from her mother. She tried to understand what was going on, and being only eleven at the time, she didn't understand all of what she was hearing ... "What do you mean you want to get married?" "You are too young!" "You are what?" "When is it due" Irma couldn't figure it all out but she knew enough to know that someone was in a lot of trouble. So relieved that it wasn't her, she soon went back to sleep.

The Need To Teach Good Things

The aged women likewise that they be in behavior as becometh holiness, not false accusers, not given to much wine, teachers of good things; that they may teach the young women to be sober, to love their husbands, to love their children. (Titus 2:3-4) kjv

Audrey and Timothy St. James were married the summer of 1939. Audrey was a month away from her eighteenth birthday, just graduating from high school with previous plans to enter college in the fall. Her husband Timothy, was only nineteen and was already enrolled in college.

They moved in with his mother, Alma, a tall, bone thin, fair complexioned sanctified widow, originally from one of the Islands off South Carolina. She had to be one of the most vindictive and sanctimonious women in the world. She loved her son so much that there was not a female around that she felt was good enough for him, certainly not Audrey. Alma had even indicated during one of her eruptions, that she was sure this baby was not even Timothy's, and that she was just trying to entrap him. She would sit and stare at Audrey and her coldness could make one shiver. Alma did all of the cleaning and cooking. Alma made it clear that *she* was not allowed in the kitchen except to eat.

Audrey would try to stay out of her way, busying herself with making little clothes for the baby. Most days, she would walk the three blocks to her parents house, spend the day dreading the time to come when she had to leave to return to that *mausoleum* where she lived. She would always get the evil eye from Alma upon her return home.

Miss Alma always kept her head covered when she went out of the apartment, and always wore long dresses and cotton stockings. People who knew her generally avoided her because she was always preaching or prophesying at them or bad mouthing her daughter-in-law. She loved her son so much that there was not a female around that she felt was really good enough for him, even Loretta, certainly not Audrey Foster, a Baptist, no less! She raked and scraped every penny to insure he finished his education.

Timothy's father had left while he was still a toddler. People who knew them said he had told her he was going into the service during the war, but when he never returned after the war, the war department eventually declared him dead. A lot of people believed he was still alive or maybe he preferred death rather than returning to such a sour lemon of a wife. After many years of living as a widow, Alma had become a very lonely and untrusting woman with few nice comments about anyone or anything.

Timothy's mother had always wanted him to marry someone like … their pastor's daughter, Loretta May. She never made a secret of it, and would invite Loretta to dinner every chance she got so that she could point out all of her good qualities to Audrey. How "virtuous Loretta was and how she was saving herself for marriage". In reality, Timothy never carried a torch for Loretta and although he was not that happy to be already married and a father, he did want to do his best for Audrey.

Alma would always direct Timothy to sit next to Loretta, at the dinner table, leaving Audrey to sit across from the two of them. Loretta was a tall, willowy, fair complexioned girl with long coarse sandy hair and a talent for the piano.

Knowing that Audrey played the piano very well, Alma still delighted herself to brag openly of Loretta's musical forte, and talked of how she had always wished they would have been able someday to marry and have beautiful and talented children. Guessing, she figured since she was a preacher's daughter, it would make a big difference. It didn't matter that Timothy had chosen to marry Audrey, who was just as talented musically. She had played piano since she was old enough to reach the keys. She had Ellien to thank for that.

Timothy resented his mother's hurtful remarks and put downs about Audrey, her way of dressing, cooking, and anything else she thought of. Alma insisted on doing her son's laundry because "she didn't want her son looking dingy"meaning she didn't like the way Audrey did his shirts. According to Audrey, they were the nit-pickiest people you'd ever want to meet but she loved Timothy.

Audrey went to work in a cookie factory, when the baby was two months old. The problems with her mother-in-law continued to escalate. Alma felt that she should have control of Audrey's income since she was Timothy's wife. Submission was the term she'd used referring Audrey to many scriptures in the Bible. Audrey assured her that would not be the case. The last straw emerged one morning when Alma had proceeded to not only verbally but physically punish her for accidently breaking her prized water pitcher that she kept in the icebox. Audrey had been up with a colicky, crying baby most of the night, while Timothy and Alma slept. She was in no mood to hear or feel his mother's banter that morning. Over Alma's screams of objections, predictions, and prophecies, she packed what she could carry in her arms, took her baby girl, and went back home to her Mama and Daddy. That was the end of her sentence at the St. James house.

Irma was confused about all of this marriage stuff when Audrey moved back in with the family, she noticed that Audrey would be crying every night and this went on for about a year. Finally Hilton had heard enough and encouraged Audrey to enroll in college. "Girl, go to school, make something of yourself!" he chided her. She took her father's advice and went. Irma was thrilled at the prospect of taking care of her little niece, Maggie. It was a happy time in her life.

Although Audrey had gotten over her breakup with Timothy, and had gone on to obtain a Doctorate in Psychology, was a college professor for thirty years, and was well traveled, she never remarried.

The last time she had seen Timothy was at their daughter Maggie's wedding. He looked so frail and weak, his wife held on to enable him to even stand up straight. He was suffering from cirrhosis of the liver and had been hospitalized for several months. He had also been in out of several detoxification centers in New York and New Jersey. His doctors had done all that they could for him. The sad part of this is that he had put his success as a college professor at the helm. After he and Audrey were divorced, his personal life had been one series of liaisons after another, until he became terminally ill. His mental state was such that, he didn't even seem to recognized his own daughter, or anyone else for that matter, except Audrey, and he kept softly murmuring what sounded like her name throughout the wedding ceremony. Although he did reconcile with his mother and joined the church, he was so ill he was admitted to a sanitarian shortly after the wedding. He died three months later.

Maggie had graduated from Syracuse University School of Broadcasting and was now a news anchor in Toronto, Ontario, and her husband Gregory, was a television news producer. They had met at an affiliate station in Quebec, where she was working as an intern. He was twenty years her senior, and successful. They met, fell in love and a month later, they were married and in barely three years had three lovely daughters Kyla, Simal, and Tihera. The circle was complete as far as they were concerned. She still kept in touch with her Aunt Irma although it was becoming difficult to communicate over the telephone. She and Jenni, seven years her junior, barely knew each other but when they visited it was always a very happy time for everyone. As time went by Maggie's daughters would sometime write to Caron and include photographs of their vacations, especially when they were in the Caribbean Islands with their grandparents during the summer. They even sent souvenirs of straw dolls and mystery boxes. They had even invited Caron on one of their summer jaunts. Their father owned a resort down in Bermuda that had been bequeathed to him from an uncle who was a merchant marine, and had literally won this resort in a poker game with one of the exclusive multimillionaires living there. It was not cruel that he had won it from this man because that man had so much money that he probably didn't even miss it. It made Gregory very content to know that his wife and daughters had solid security in case something were to happen to him.

CHAPTER 7

Things Of Good Rapport

"Whatsoever things are true, whatsoever things are honest whatsoever things are just, whatsoever things are pure, whatsoever things are lovely, whatsover things are of good report; if there be any virtue, and if there be any praise, think on these things." (Phil. 4:8)

Royal Lewis Dobbson, Jr. nicknamed Roy for short, was not always as enthusiastic about church activities as Irma was, maybe because he was born the son of a Primitive Baptist preacher, and the daughter of a traveling missionary. They came from a long line of preachers, at least three generations.

Roy, the eldest of seven children, was raised on a farm in Eastward, a small farming town northwest of Savannah, Georgia, and spent at least three days of the week in church whether he wished to be there or not. His dad would insist that the whole family and his grandmother, all ten of them, pile into their old clunker with a packed dinner basket on Sunday morning, prepared to spend the whole day under the big elms that surrounded the small white clapboard church.

There was no air conditioning or electric fans, just the old cardboard fans that were fashioned by the ladies on the Usher Board, so the trees were a valuable asset. One thing Irma did remember was that they had a serious relationship with God.

Irma was only twelve at the time and had come from Newark to spend the summer with her cousin, Remelle Hodges, and they had sat in the very back of the church near the door in their stiffly starched eyelet dresses and black patent leather vaseline polished pumps, giggling silently to themselves, critiquing every young man walking in. They would quietly snicker at some of the boys like Gus Lane and Jackie Chambers who were just dazzled, meeting a pretty little city girl like Irma. They lived down the street from Remelle and were always trying to talk to them. Gus had a lot of acne, and Jackie had bad breath, a big gap in his front teeth and a bad haircut. His mother used to cut his hair with her scissors and a soup bowl, or so the rumor had it; anyway, she thought he looked weird. She noticed Roy because He was so tall, neatly dressed, sparkling white teeth, and rather handsome in a goofy sort of way. He was somewhat shy but friendly. He sensed they were watching him but he did not dare turn around.

After services were over one Sunday, he finally asked Remelle about her cousin. Irma pretended not to notice, carefully striding right pass them heading for the picnic table where her aunt Shirlene, had set a place for the three of them. Soon Roy enticed by Remelle, came over and sat at their table and had dinner with them. Aunt Shirlene always brought a ton of fried chicken, potato salad, and sliced cake, just in case.

Shirlene Flood Hodges was a widow. She had been married to Ellien's brother, Jamison Hodges, a ship cabin steward. He had been killed in an explosion on a ship that was enroute to Alaska. The War Department had paid Shirlene a lump sum death benefit and provided for her and Remelle who was a very young toddler at the time, a monthly widow's pension. Ellien and Shirlene were very close friends growing up and they remained close after all of those years. Ellien knew how much Shirlene had loved Jamison and how much she missed him. She was the only person, they would have allowed Irma to spend that much time with, away from home.

During these Sunday after church picnics, they would gather in groups and laugh and talk until one of the old sisters would ask them if they knew their commandments. She would always give a handful of jellybeans to the one who recited correctly most of the Ten Commandments without stopping. Irma and Remelle never won because Janie, one of Roy's sisters would

40

always recite them perfectly so she always got the jelly beans. The other reason was that Irma and Remelle were more occupied with keeping an eye on Roy, and trying to keep Gus and Jackie out of their hair.

Jackie was an only child, and a real pest. He and his mom lived in an old house down at the end of Wright River Road, they had no electricity, so Jackie had to be in and have all of the kerosene lamps lit before sundown, otherwise they would be stranded in the dark. Gus lived two houses away from Remelle. His mother and father worked for the Yuri Kasselbaums, a Jewish couple who had come down from New York City about twenty years before to open a department store, the first of its kind in that part of the state.

They sold everything from shoelaces to sling-shots, from lace to burlap bags. They had a book that they called a credit ledger, and they were the first people to even think about giving the colored people in that town any kind of merchandise on credit. Aunt Shirlene never used this book to get anything on credit, she never trusted these people in the first place and she was not about to be "obliged" as she put it, to anyone, especially white folks.

It was rumored that the Kasselbaums were quite wealthy, but to every one around they appeared to be very stingy with money. They would give you on credit, the outdated stuff like old moldy clothing on shelves that just didn't sell. If you had cash, they would let you pick out the nice stuff. Aunt Shirlene and Remelle always got the nice stuff; because they paid cash for it.

The Kasselbaums would never buy more food than what they could eat in a day, so Dolly cooked fresh for them every day, and sneaked the leftovers securely down in her bosom and under her apron to take home. Since the Kasselbaums were Orthodox Jews, in their observance, every Friday at sundown, the lights and everything was turned off in their home and store. They did nothing from sundown Friday until sundown Saturday.

Being Jewish the Kasselbaums never celebrated Christmas and that was always an amazement to Remelle, who could hardly contain her excitement as she and her mother poured over all of the beautiful things she dreamed of seeing under that tree on Christmas morning. *"These people don't even have a tree, Momma! just a big old candle stand with some candles that don't even match!* "she complained to her mother as they walked out. "That is a menorrah Remelle, they celebrate Hanukkah. I will explain it to you when we get home, okay?" Just then an old white man, Burford Sholar (a known Klansman), passed them and spat tobacco juice, nearly hitting Shirlene's foot. She just kept walking because in those days, that is what you did, if you wanted to stay alive in the south. Many lynchings, and cross burnings had taken place in this region infested with KKK activities. They had even threatened the Kasselbaums for being so civil to coloreds but old Mr. Kasselbaum didn't change, he understood. Aunt Shirlene detested all of them, including the Kasselbaums.

The Lanes were the first family to get a double sink and an electric range for the kitchen, and it was a three burner with a deep-well top. Everyone in the neighborhood dropped by to *"see that stove."* Gus' mother, Dolly Lane, was the Kasselbaum's cook and housekeeper, and Gus' father, Augustus Faulkner Lane, Jr. did yard work, repairs around the house, and drove Mrs. Kasselbaum back and forth in that big black car, wherever she needed to go. It was rumored that Mrs. Kasselbaum had some kind of disease, but they didn't know what it was. They figured it was something that only rich white people caught. She had such yellow skin and always smelled like sulfur whenever she returned from the doctor. No one dared ask her.

Aunt Shirlene and Dolly always sat on the back porch swing, in the evening and talked about everything that went on with everybody, everywhere, including the single school teacher who lived in the third house down, and never came out of her house during the day for anything or anyone. She was quite strange, everyone thought. It seems that she had been jilted by a man and since that time, she became a recluse and her only visitor was someone who visited late at night. Who he was they never knew. At least they never called him by name.

Remelle warned Irma never to ask that question about grown persons to any grown-ups. She knew better because she had already been slapped in the mouth for asking questions like that. Aunt Shirlene didn't play. One time Remelle had made the error of asking her mother how Sister Vanessa's daughter, Niecie, had "broken her leg" again? It seemed she broke it once before, but Remelle couldn't figure why there was no splint or anything, and the very next Sunday, she was at church walking just fine and carrying a baby. It wasn't worth getting hit that hard in the mouth again for being curious, so she wanted to make sure Irma didn't find herself in bad trouble like that. If grownups were talking, they knew they had better not listen openly, it was better for them to hide under the house where it was cool and in perfect ear shot.

They would walk everyday down the shaded lane to the mail box by the road to see if there was a letter for Irma from home, and then Aunt Shirlene would sometimes drive them into town in her big shiny new car. It was a nineteen thirty nine Ford. People didn't really like Aunt Shirlene that much because she had real nice things, and some of them were jealous. They couldn't figure how she could afford that car and not even work. Aunt Shirlene didn't care what people said about her, she had bought that car after her dad died and left two large insurance polices. She also had a large gramophone and lots of seventy-eight RPM records and at night they would listen to Sister Rosetta Thorpe, The Blind Boys, and some of the other gospel greats.

Shirlene's father, Ira Flood was a brick mason, the Worshipful Master in his Masonic Lodge, and a deacon in Roy's father's church. Soon after Shirlene's mother passed on, he married one of the lady ushers at church, Sister Lois Mae Cheney, a snuff dipping middle aged woman who wore wigs and stiff starched white usher uniforms. He was looking for someone to replace his late wife; someone to wash, iron, and cook for him. She was available, had never been married before and she was just waiting for someone to propose to her at least once in her life time. It was rumored that Sister Lois Mae had a lot of money, but no one would dare ask her if the rumors were true. She was not a person you would approach with a question like that if you wanted to keep peace, it would be to your detriment, if you dared get into her business, which didn't say much for her as a Christian woman.

She lived in a very big white house, kept the shades down day and night; drove a big gray car and always wore low-cut Bamberg dresses when she wasn't in uniform. It was said by some that her father had fought in the civil war, and some said he had been a buffalo soldier; and somehow he had managed to find a large sum of money while his squad was hiding out on maneuvers, and instead of turning the money in to his unit, he managed to pack it all over his body, in his boots, and in his bunk mattress until he got a release from the Army. He kept all of it, bought as much land as he could, farmed it, and when he died left everything to his daughter, Lois Mae.

She and Shirlene kept their distance from each other. Shirlene lived in her parents home, and her father lived with his new wife in her home. Shirlene would go and pick her father up and bring him to her house to visit but she never went inside Sister Cheney's house. She didn't think it would be right. She felt like that would dishonor her mother's memory to do that, and anyway, that house always looked so dark inside. "There's just no telling what goes on in that house" she mused.

Shirlene's father was about seventy-nine years old when he died from pneumonia, he had wondered out the house in the freezing cold late one night trying to go back to his old house, and somehow he got confused and wondered into some woods. Sister Cheney didn't miss him until the next morning. When they found him, he was frost bitten and suffering from hypothermia. They took him into the house, put him in a tub of water and tried to warm him up but by then he was too sick. A week later Shirlene's father died from the consumption. No one even realized that he had already displayed symptoms of dementia for many years.

Aunt Shirlene dressed Irma and Remelle in nice starched dresses, patent leather shoes, and matching ribbons in their hair for church even during the weeknight services, and she'd drive them in her car down the road to the church a little early, giving them an opportunity to establish their positions so they missed nothing. Deacon Joe Nesbitt, Jackies's uncle, would unlatch the door for them, so that they could sit in the vestibule where it was cool, and watch everyone come in. He would enjoy listening as they'd recite Bible verses that they had learned in Sunday school. Deacon Nesbitt couldn't read or write very well but he always knew if the verses they recited were correct. He knew the "Word" by memory. Irma somehow now recalled the Sunday that she and Remelle went up to the front of the church and sat on the two chairs that Reverend Dobbson referred to in his sermon as the "*mourning bench*" and they joined the church, accepting Christ as their "Personal Savior."

They were now "saints". All of this made sense to Irma except the part when she was informed that they were to be immediately baptized in that creek down behind the church. That barefoot walk down the path to the creek was a very long one for these two girls.

There were rumors of catfish and moccasins residing in that lake and it frightened her silly just thinking about it. Irma had always been afraid of snakes and spiders, and just hearing all of the stories about them made her pretty nervous. She was thinking about the time her Uncle Walter showed them his scar where he had been bitten on the arm by a five foot long diamondback rattler while picking blackberries in the patch behind their house. Mr. Rufus had sucked out the poison, grabbed a pint of moonshine, poured a little on the wound and drank the rest; wrapped the arm with a clean rag and rushed him over to Doctor Smith who was a veterinarian. He treated them and their horses, because there were no doctors around who would take coloreds as patients, unless they worked in the houses as cooks or maids. All of this happening so fast brought back some frightening thoughts for little Irma Foster that day while standing on the banks of that creek. At one point she felt she needed to rethink this whole situation, maybe this decision was made in a little too much haste. She wondered what Robert James would have done in a case like this. She missed him now.

Aunt Shirlene made sure they were well wrapped in those sheets and a plastic covering for their hair. When it was over they walked shivering back to the church singing an old time spiritual *"I Know I Got Religion, Cause I been baptized!"*

All of this was new for Irma because the church back in Newark had a big tub behind the pulpit and the water was warm. She wondered why these people would rather go to a creek rather than put a big tub in back of their church? She soon figured it wasn't worth worrying about, especially since Aunt Shirlene had dried both of them very careful and helped them to get dressed all pretty again. She was too excited about spending the rest of that afternoon with Roy. She was really infatuated with this young man, and he really liked her too.

They soon began sitting together in church and afterward they would stand under the big trees and talk until Aunt Shirlene cleared her throat, as a signal meaning it was time for her to get into the car and head for home. At the end of her summer stay, they were already at the hand holding stage, and he finally got up enough nerve to ask for her address. Irma was so tickled just thinking of getting a real letter from this boy. She dreaded going back home after the wonderful summer she had spent in Eastward.

After that summer, and all the summers to follow for the next five years, Irma was allowed to come and stay at Aunt Shirlene's and during the other times she and Roy kept in touch by writing long letters. Those were the days. She could almost smell the aroma of the frying chicken in her aunt's kitchen on Sunday mornings and the anticipation of lending her hand to crank the ice cream churn until it became so stiff they'd have to remove the dasher. Oh, how good that ice cream tasted sliding down her dry throat on those hot Sunday afternoons. She would sometimes eat as many as three saucers full, and end up with a terrible stomach ache and have to drink that awful bicarbonate of soda that Aunt Shirlene would mix up. It tasted terrible and Aunt Shirlene said that was their punishment for their "eyes being bigger than their bellies."

After high school, Roy went to Delaware to attend college, on a scholarship that he had received. Two years later, Irma enrolled in a college near Baltimore, just a short distance away. They dated each other steadily until Roy came out of college. Back in those days, to go that far away to college was like going to the moon. Everyone showed up at the bus station to see Roy off to school, wishing him well and some even pressing a few coins in his palm as they hugged him and shook his hand. Some of the women brought so many shoe boxes of fried chicken and teacakes for his trip, he had to get a box from Mr. Kasslebaum's store to check some of it as luggage. When he arrived at school everyone in the building knew what he had because that chicken was smelling up every piece of clothing he wore for the first week. Some of the college jocks teased him about the chicken, but after he offered to share it, they became good friends.

When the Korean War grew strong Roy, entered the military to serve his draft commitment. They were so afraid that Roy would be sent overseas, but he was blessed to be able to stay back. The first furlough weekend he earned after boot camp, he came down from Camp Dix for the weekend, and the two of them ran off and eloped in a courthouse ceremony in Bel Aire, Maryland. You did not have to go through a long procedure in Maryland to marry in those days, so they were able to get married in one afternoon, spend their honeymoon holding hands on the back of the bus headed for New Jersey, and rent an efficiency apartment across from his camp, all in one long weekend.

Irma was not allowed to go with him because he had to be in his barracks, and the area where he had to live was segregated. He had not even gotten permission from the Army to marry. She could lie in her bed each morning and hear them marching and cadences being called as troops

47

kept time with their drill sergeants. Most of her time was spent pacing back and forth trying to figure out what she should say to her parents. She knew they would have to tell her parents and soon. At nineteen years of age, she knew they would be so upset, for they had always wanted Irma to become a teacher, since she was always playing school with her brothers and she demanded to be the "teacher" each time. That would all have to be put on hold now. Irma had a husband to take care of. She rolled over and slept. Later in the day she would walk along the large fence hoping to get a glance of Roy, and she waited breathlessly for their weekends to come.

Roy would sneak pass the guards while a friend of his provided a distraction, and visit Irma, and on Sundays, they would attend chapel services at the colored chapel on post together, easily blending in with the rest of the families, smiling and squeezing each other's hand tightly as they sat through some of the most boring sermons they ever had to endure. It made Roy a little homesick for his father's sermons after all. They knew they had to tell their parents soon. They used his next weekend pass to travel to Newark to inform her parents. They did not take this news well. After that it was necessary to inform Roy's parents, so they wrote a letter.

CHAPTER 8

The Unexpected Comes as A Thief

Irma's mind started wandering back to the time that Jenni was born. Like viewing a motion picture in her mind, she remembered that she and Roy had been married for a year and a half when Jennifer Marie, their little baby girl was born. She was indeed a gift from God. They were ecstatic and by now she and Roy had a nice little upstairs apartment off post, having finished all of his training. They began their real home life together. Two years later, they and their beautiful baby girl moved into their all new freshly built Suburban Maryland tract home and began, what was still quite vivid in Irma's mind a very warm and loving family life. Irma and Roy were making plans for their second child, but that was not to be.

Irma had been feeling a lot of indigestion for the past few nights and her neighbor, full of myths and suspicions, had told her "that means that baby is coming here with a full head of hair!" and then advised her to drink a little bicarbonate before lying down. So realizing she was out of it, Irma walked the half mile to the corner grocery store to buy a box. On her way back, she heard a commotion and when she turned around to see who was running, two young boys came sprinting past her being chased by three policemen. In the process of trying to get out of the way, one of the policemen ran right across her path, knocking Irma nearly senseless and to the pavement, right on her back, yelling "Move! hurry up! get out of my way!" Irma tried to get to her feet but the weight of her pregnancy prevented her. A man sitting on his front porch who had witnessed it all, picked her up and helped her to the chair, but she seemed unable to stand and was in severe pain. Already in her seventh month, she started labor. By the time the ambulance arrived she had started to hemorrhage severely, she had suffered a pelvic fracture. They rushed her to the hospital but by the time they got her into surgery it was too late for the little baby boy. The doctor told Roy that the baby was still-born, as a result of the ruptured placenta, and loss of oxygen. Due to the severity of the pelvic injury, Irma would never bear more children. They were devastated. Roy and Irma named their son Royal Lewis Dobbson, the third. Nothing was ever done about the policeman who had knocked her to the ground. He never even apologized. Irma knowing she would never have another child, promised God she would do her best to raise, teach, and nourish Jenni, to become everything that she is to her mother right now.

Losing touch of reality, nothing seems real, and nothing is the same anymore. What a person could at one time do without thinking, now warrants much study.

Irma remembered her lost baby son now. Why was she thinking of him? She sat back in her chair, closing her eyes, crying softly, and singing softly:

> *"I look around, I shake my head,*
> *Something was taken from me,*
> *An empty space, lost days, a year*
> *Oh yes, a thief was here*
> *I keep drifting from my present*
> *Fading back to my past*
> *A bough was broken*
> *A twig suddenly snapped,*
> *My life, my youth seems to*
> *Woo me, waving, parading by.*
> *I must hold tight what is left,*
> *I know some things are strange,*
> *Things I do, and things I say.*

Now as Irma sat silently, nearly fifty years later, vaguely remembering these happy times, she tried to make sense of the confusion and fear surrounding her now. How had all of this happened, why was she alone now? Why was she so forgetful?

She had drawn her bath water earlier and now it sat cold in the bathtub, she wondered why there was so much water in the tub? Who is going to use it, maybe Jenni was going to bring the kids over and put them to bed, so the bath water was for them? Then she remembered she was supposed to use it. She stood there looking at the ripples and all of a sudden things started to rotate in her mind and she was back at school again.

Her mind took her back to Mrs. Walsh, her fifth grade music teacher, and how she stood over her with the ruler to tap her on her knuckles each time she counted numbers on her fingers, "Tisch ... Irma Jean Forest, do not count on your fingers! You must recite from memory!" Mrs. Walsh would say as she perused out of her corner eye, other papers on other desks.

Mrs. Walsh was very strict, yet gentle and all of her students loved her. She had taught Audrey, Earnest, and several of her cousins. She would often reward her students with a shiny red apple each Friday, having them delivered to her classroom just before recess. Irma wondered for a minute why she remembered this so clearly now? Why is it that when she thinks of people she knew they are no longer around? Even Miss Moss, her fifth grade piano teacher, that was such a boring class to Irma because she lived with the piano daily at home. She tried to concentrate on the things she must accomplish today.

By now she recalled where she had "put up her tools" and she retrieved them and decided to go and weed her flower garden, she knew that the garden has always been a sort of therapy to her. As she worked in the warm morning sun, Irma sang softly to herself, recalling the era of her youth and days of long ago, like when she and Robert James would climb the hill and go over the trestle to watch the trains go by carrying all of those well dressed people. They all seemed to be talking and laughing, she and Robert James sat wondering where they were going and dreaming of the day when they would be able to go somewhere on that pretty train. It seems these events were clearer in her mind than current events.

Lost in the Fifties

Once she had even gone to the storage shed, taking Jenni's old bicycle from the rack and attempted to ride it around the block. Unfortunately she wasn't very lucky at that as she had fallen off, landing on a culvert scraping her face, hands and shoulder. Her next door neighbor, Mamie (probably one of the nosiest people in the world) had yelled, "Be careful on that bicycle, Miss Irma you are no spring chicken! You haven't rode a bike in over fifty years!" Irma had decided to just ignore such a comment, to her own peril. There was a desperate look of bewilderment on Irma's face as Mamie helped her to the front door and then telephoned Jenni.

Mamie sat in her window all of the time just looking and listening for any little tidbit that she might get to gossip about. She was a very lonely widow, who missed her husband, and children. Her daughter lived in New Jersey with her husband and four children, and her son was in the Air Force stationed in Japan. Her daughter rarely visited because they were always "busy", and her son she only saw about every two or three years.

Jenni hung up the telephone, rushed right over and immediately began scolding her mother for doing ridiculous things like that, knowing how dangerous it is. She was becoming more and more impatient with some of the antics Irma would pull from time to time and she figured it was Irma's way of getting attention.

She knew her mother would never leave her home to come and live with her, but she also knew that her mother was getting more and more unreliable as the days went by. How long would it be before she wandered off someplace and got lost ... Jenni thought. Somehow she would soon have to develop some kind of care plan for her mother because she knew it was only a matter of time before something she prayed not tragic would happen in her absence. All she could do was pray about this serious situation. She did not look forward to becoming her own mother's parent. That was a reverse role she definitely did not desire.

CHAPTER 9

A Kingdom Called Confusion

The time comes in the lives of many parents when they are almost totally reversed in their pattern of parental behavior. The child is now assuming all of the responsibilities of what parents assumed as they grew up. Having to supervise their getting up, washing up, going to bed routine that seemed to run like a well oiled machine when we were young, now seems to be a very stressful and sensitive task.

We are not comfortable giving what we used to so easily take; i.e. instructions. Even in the best of circumstances that element of parental honor or intimidation still somehow grips us with the fear of being disrespectful if we must admonish the very person who had a vital part of shaping us into what we have become today. It is a strange and chilly feeling like searching for a candle in the dark, finding it and then having a bad match, we become frightened, bewildered, and there erupts a kingdom called "confusion".

Perhaps the most bewildering thought is "the lost of faith". People who have exhibited spiritual strength and have been champions for reaching the lost and teaching the found all of a sudden cannot even remember the Lord's prayer. Irma would sometimes kneel for an hour before she could remember what she wanted to pray about. It was all so frustrating, so frightening to her. She would see her Bible laying next to her bed and when she tried to read verses, she just could not concentrate. She didn't understand why. Only God.

One of the first things Jenni had to do was to get Irma to a doctor for a thorough exam to find out if there were any physical problems such as tumors, respiratory or circulatory problems present. Other than general aging factors, there were no serious health problems. Next a CAT Scan, EKG, MRI, and blood work were done. A Neurologist and a Psychologist examined her for both brain damage and trauma, conjecture: what preceded this change of behavior, was it a sudden, gradual or on-going condition. Irma was suffering from what is called Alzheimer disease.

There are many symptoms and characteristics to identify Alzheimer disease. And sometimes there are none. One of the specialist recommended that Jenni hire someone to sit with her mother during the day (Managed Care), and a therapist, so that she could continue to lead a somewhat normal life. Irma would not hear of it. "I don't want people coming into my home taking things from me. I don't trust this person, that person, etc." she would rant. Jenni would just throw her hands up in the air helplessly, "Mom I don't know what I am going to do with you! You know that I wouldn't allow someone I didn't trust to be here!" "But you don't know these people, Jennifer! They are trying to hurt me!" Her mother would insist.

Jenni explored many options and possibilities concerning her mother's care as there wasn't a lot of information on Alzheimer disease available to the public at that time. About a month after her mother's accident, Jenni ran into a long time friend and classmate, Frankie Lockheart, whom she had not seen or talked to for several years, she was so excited to see her and "why hadn't they gotten together for so long" as the usual greetings and commentaries go; she discovered that her friend, now divorced, had been out of circulation due to caring for her aged parents. Her father had suffered from Alzheimer for over fifteen years, and recently, her mother had been diagnosed with Dementia, which is also a form of Alzheimer.

She explained to Jenni over lunch how her mother had been her husband's care giver for several years and refused any outside help, (Skilled Care), her attitude was "We don't have to let the world know our private lives." But as time went by, she began losing control, her husband became combative and insolent. She get hit if he didn't like something. There were times she would prepare food and as soon as she would serve it to him he would go into a fitful rage and toss everything into the sink accusing her of trying to poison him. In the meantime, she was getting more and more confused not knowing what to do with him, whether to get help or try to weather the storm with him herself.

Frankie's mother was already forgetting little details like locking doors and keeping the keys in a place where she could find them. Once she came home from the grocery store to find her husband stripped down to his underwear, evidence of a failed bathroom visit, painting their couch with green paint, (the original color of the couch was light beige). Another time while doing the laundry, he attempted to "help her" by pouring a gallon of bleach into the washer and ruining a load of her best linens. The house was so full of garbage and trash, unopened mail, sour milk containers, old molded food, you name it, it was there. Their life was one shining example of what this dreadful condition effuses.

There was no reasoning with him, he was insolent and other times completely introverted (Demented). "What could she do with this formerly gentle and kind man of his youth who had now turned into a complete stranger, afraid to lie down and sleep at night unless all of the lights were on and the television blasting?" This man, a well-known, successful, retired pharmacist, who was so allegiant, now refuses to even take medicine that is vital to his health or even a good hot bath.

These problems continued for years, with enough incidents and accidents to write a book of wonders, their once warm and friendly home was slowly turning into a house of chimeras, with the cleaning, laundry, meals, and other duties, her mother was swamped. Yet, she still refused outside help because she didn't want people to know their "shame".

Alzheimer's crippling, degenerative condition crosses every border and culture, and racial divide; invading many lives, displaying so many characteristics, demeanor, and individualities that it is difficult to address this condition as one size fits all. [This is spoken in a layman's terms.]

Frankie had to assume total responsibility for both parents after receiving a call from the police one day that her father had locked her mother out of the house as she stepped out to get the mail wearing only a sweater, the temperature was below zero and he refused to let her back in "he never let strangers into the house" he kept telling her all the while he was sitting on their painted couch with the remote control. Finally, a neighbor down the street noticed that she was out there crouched on the steps for so long, trying to keep from freezing, she had come over and offered assistance. Finally they were able to get the door open just short of her mom suffering severe frost bite on her fingers and toes (she was wearing only bath slippers on her feet) and when they did get in he became combative. They had no choice but to call the police.

He was so much stronger than the two of them, they had trouble restraining him, he even bit the neighbor severely. It must be understood, that he did not know what he was doing and he was gripped with fear by the time his daughter arrived. She was even a stranger to him.

Frankie quit her teaching job and moved in with them, hired a housekeeper, and began to assist in their care. By this time her mom had developed a congestive heart failure, and was told by her doctor she would have to maintain a strict regimented diet and exercise program, consequently, her daughter now will take up where mom left off. Mom and dad both required skilled nursing care on a daily basis.

Jenni's having met Frankie that day was the turning point in their lives. She had no idea that her friend had been going through all of this for so long. For Jenni to discover that Frankie had had to stop living her life so that they could continue living theirs had a very sobering effect in her decision to tackle this disorder.

In-home care is one of the most difficult tasks for families especially if they do not receive outside help. Because her father did not have a serious medical or debilitating physical condition, it would prove to be a real struggle for her to get home care assistance for her father. She would have to hire someone or be prepared to handle this herself. Fear now gripped her and she knew that was one thing she had to come to terms with immediately.

One of the dangers of living alone with someone who suffers from this disease, one who tends to become combative, confused over a small inconvenience or difficulty. They have lost their ability to rationalize and the fear of losing further control of their lives drives this anger in them. Fear drives them to wander around searching for something they think they may have lost, when it is only misplaced. Fear that someone is stealing from them or plotting to harm them.

The paranoia of being abandoned causes them to cling to loved ones (or resist them). They have become suspicious of everyone and everything then there are the ones who are just the opposite; the ones who stop communicating altogether. The symptoms have nothing to do with their intellect. Many Alzheimer patients were clergy, teachers, nurses, even physicians.

If they are speaking, the memory starts to fade and they become very confused, unable to finish a sentence. They may be asked a question and the answer might not come for several minutes or hours. Then there is also a chance, they may never answer.

There are incidences of people relating events where the patient was asked a question months ago, and all of a sudden, out of the blue, they'll provide a sensible answer, unfortunately by this time one may have forgotten the question.

All of the factors play a role in the atmosphere of their lives. Jenni was more and more concerned for Irma because she still talked to everyone, including strangers. Would she become a target for some unscrupulous con artist, door to door sales-person, or even a "not-so-honest-friend"?

They are sometimes preyed upon by persons they really think that they can trust. It is not always the family member they'll trust. They sometime stop trusting the family member or immediate family care giver first. For some unknown reason, the resentment of the reverse role. Parent - child then child - parent dance is greatly disapproved in many situations by both child and the parent, but most assuredly the parent. They have always been in control now the very person they controlled has to supervise (control them). It is a dreadful feeling of lost, a twilight zone.

A generation of gaps and faded memories in the present era surfaces, while they sometime have the abilities to return to their youth and give you a complete dissertation of the new Studebaker their father purchased or the stock market crash depression of the thirties. Their grade school teachers, Sunday school teachers, childhood pals, now replace the grandchildren, children, and friends of their present generation. They sometime even forget how to pray. They kneel next to their bed but can't remember what to say, worse yet, they may not even remember how to get up off of their knees. They remove their clothing and carefully fold each piece perfectly, carefully placing each piece in a place where they can be easily located. They try very hard to avoid confusion, misplacement, they are fighting a losing battle of control. One can only imagine what is going on in the minds of the Alzheimer patient.

A very important point to add - many suffer for years ... in silence.

Jenni decided to read and research all of the information available to her. She knew that it was only a matter of time before she would be faced with the same situation her friend Frankie had faced. There was little getting around it. She knew that education and prayers would be her saving grace. Irma had very early in Jenni's life instilled by example, in her a deep faith in God, so now Jenni would have to really put her faith to the test. She had to start the engine of this machine now!

CHAPTER 10

It's The Open Window - Under Which We Stand

As Jenni reflected on the various situations and the decisions facing her now, she had a peace in her spirit knowing that her most important obligation was in tact, that is, her personal relationship with God. This relationship was a guide and a consolation when faced with any adversities, and she had many during this time dealing with her mother. She remembered the scriptures that her mother used to read daily, one of them was found in James 5:16bkjv (The effectual fervent prayer of a righteous man availeth much.) and now she understood well what Irma had been saying to her, after all these years. She thanked God for a mother who prayed while she could. It was a smart investment, for now was the time and the situation at hand.

During the years Jenni and Jim were married, most weekends were spent doing all sorts of recreational activities. Saturdays would be spent on music lessons, shopping and running errands with Caron and Jimmy, after which they'd all go out for pizza and maybe see a movie. Sundays, the family would go to early morning Sunday school and worship service, have brunch then spend the rest of the day at the lake or country club swimming and playing tennis.

The children seemed to grow up so fast, Jenni thought to herself as she drove home. She had time on her hands now that Jim was gone and Caron away in college. Caron called often, just to "check" on things. She was a lot like her father, very driven and very strong. She had always excelled in school, pre-kindergarten through twelfth grade, graduating with honors, and many scholarships. She had already been accepted at Radcliff her junior year, and the family had made a vacation of it when they visited the school and surrounding areas to see if she liked it.

They were all so proud of her. She was the apple of her dad's eye, there was nothing too good for his Caron, he used to call her his "Bunny" because she was so cute and always laughing about almost anything. She had features like her Aunt Les, her height and beauty was noticeable to everyone.

When her father died, she felt as if something had been twisted and torn out of her. She longed to see her aunt Lessie. She couldn't believe she wasn't there for the funeral, her brother's funeral. Afterwards, she locked herself in her room and cried softly in her pillow for two days. She refused to eat, and Jenni had been so worried about her. Jimmy finally convinced her to allow him to at least bring in a tray to keep her from dehydrating. Caron could not understand why this was happening and why there was so much pain. She had decided that she would try to sneak a visit to her aunt when school starts. She had many questions running around in her innocent mind. Maybe she would talk to Grandmother Irma about this, she thought.

Irma's memory of Lessie was somewhat vague, but Irma had not totally forgotten her. In her mind she recalled the first time she met Lessie, and how much she liked her, in spite of what others said about her. Irma never let the opinions of others change her opinions of people. She made the effort to know them for herself. She recalled Lessie's moxie.

CHAPTER 11

A Time Of Reconciling

Lessie glanced at herself as she passed her hall mirror on her way out of the door. The years were starting to show her age now. She never thought she could maintain her beauty forever, but now seeing the scattering of gray hairs and a few wrinkles, she felt the years, and feared her youth slipping away. No matter how much she exercised there were still areas that needed a little work. Maybe a little plastic surgery or lipo would do the trick. How long had it been? Would the children even recognize her now, they hadn't seen her in over ten years. Time seemed to have just flown by.

It had been such a wonderful vacation, swimming, lying on the beach, the warm breezy nights. She thought about the children. Maybe she could convince Jenni to encourage Caron to come and spend weekends with her since she was attending school not far away.

Lessie was Jim's younger sister, a perky, and sophisticated woman in her early-fifties. She had been educated at City College, traveled and studied in Europe, Africa, and the Middle East. She cavorted with some of the popular show business crowds in New York and in California. Lessie was the one who introduced Irma to Caviar and Escargot. She had met President Nixon, having been invited to a White House dinner, as a guest of a well known Congressman from New York. Designer edition dresses, furs, jewelry, french perfumes, you name it she wore it. There was no doubt in Lessie's mind that she was beautiful, because all of her life people constantly reminded her.

Her friends nicknamed her "Lola" because whatever she wanted, she got.

She also had explored "marriage" and tried it on for size at least four times in less than a twenty year span, all of them ending in divorce, and all of them to much older well to do men and she had the alimony checks to prove it.

She had an intense beauty about her. Upon entering a room, she would just light it up with her personality, and she loved to flirt. She had an elegance about her that women envied and men loved. She had beautiful tinted chestnut brown hair, a light golden flawless complexion, and a beautiful smile. What really turned heads was her perfect size ten, coke bottle figure always impeccably attired.

She and her brother Jim had been given the best that their parents could afford. Gordon and Empress Boyd Cason, owned a tailor shop and boutique in Harlem, fashioning suits and dresses for the well to do - such as the Cotton Club patrons and many famous musicians and entertainers. They took pains to instill power and pride in their offspring at a very early age; so when they saw something they wanted they went for it. They were very proud people.

Empress' father, Wedgewood Boyd, a very distinguished and cultivated man was one of the charter member of the "Chandeliers", an elite social club that was very popular in Washington DC. He was a very talented pastry chef in one of the kitchens at the Capital, and had met his wife to be, Senta Adams at one of the Renaissance Ladies Socials which they were allowed to hold on Sunday afternoons once a month on the back lawn. Senta was one of the dressmakers for the White House ladies at that time. She was the bi-racial daughter of a white senator and his cook from Williamsburg, Virginia, very petite and beautiful. She and her mother lived right behind the White House in one of the better servants' cottages. They were one of the first to get running water and a furnace. They lived very comfortably with their separate but equal amenities.

Gordon's parents, Somersby and Felicity Cason, came over from the Caribbean Island of Kingston, Jamaica, as newly wed immigrants, speaking beautiful Queen's English, and very quickly established themselves by working in the top grade hotels in New York. They met many well off people in those hotels and soon began to mimic these people to such an extent, to think of themselves as a cut above the rest of the workers. They refused to eat in the rear of the kitchen, with the other employees, but rather they would find an empty room or suite upstairs with a table and set it up as if they were living there.

They would spend their free time practicing formality learning all of the tricks of the trades, and became so good at it, they were eventually offered the position as housekeeper and butler for one of the mayors. They held their heads and noses higher than the other employees. Gordon was born in the servants quarters of the mayor's mansion. He was able to go to a private academy that was unusual for minorities back then.

A German Jewish Tailor named Hiram Rauchsteiner, who owned one of the city's largest haberdasheries hired Gordon to keep the shop clean, and in the process of his working there, discovered he had a talent for designing and cutting out suit patterns. His boss, was so impressed at this talent displayed by Gordon, that he took him under his wings and started teaching him the techniques of fine tailoring. By the time Gordon was twenty-one, he was cutting and making suits right next to Mr. Rauchsteiner. This proved to be a real source of big money for Gordon. When he met and married Empress, they pooled his talent and her money (she taught school) together and opened their own haberdashery. This was the first of that kind up in Harlem.

Their customers were-well-to-do whites who liked and demanded their quality workmanship. Not only did they get some of the top classed customers, they refused to service their own race of people in some circumstances. They had to look and act like they could afford this service before Empress would cut one piece of cloth for them. Empress was a very meticulous lady, ran their business well, thus, they lost very few customers and rarely dealt with deadbeats who never paid for ordered merchandise. This afforded them a beautiful townhouse in Harlem decorated with beautiful furnishings, a life of comfort, and one that would provide well financially for Jim and Lessie's education at one of the prestigious private Catholic schools nearby. They placed themselves in the category known as "The Better-thans" because they had a little money. Unfortunately there were few spiritual riches in their lives. Thank God Jim had married someone like Jenni whose sound examples eventually won him to make a sound decision to accept Christ very early in the marriage. He had been brought up in a part Episcopal-part Baptist household with no real emphasis on either. His parents were just too busy all week so Sundays they needed to rest and going to church would take too much time from their day. They only attended on the CEM days (Christmas, Easter, Mother's Day) when all of the high society members came in their worsted wools and minks.

Jim and Lessie were close as brother and sister. Jim was always a bit over protective of his sister, as far as the men in her life. He knew that Lessie loved living on the edge. He did not approve of most of her choices. She had the dubious distinction of being known as a "Femme Fatale."

It was during their last vacation together that she had one indiscretion too many. Jenni and Jim's Pastor's young son, Avery, a second year college student who looked like he was at least twenty-five, caught Lessie's eye. Once she saw him, she lost complete control of herself, and her senses.

Life Is Short - After all

She made the mistake of inviting him to her very private suite, and he was discovered exiting it around five-thirty the next morning, just as Jim was coming out to meet Avery's father for an early morning jog along the beach. One can only imagine the surprised look on his father's face, not to mention the horror on Jim's. Avery was supposed to be sharing a room with two of the other boys, instead, she had managed to reel him in after hours. Needless to say, Jim completely exiled her from his family and would not speak of her, or allow her name to be spoken in his home. He felt that she had embarrassed him by her antics, and he declared that he would never forgive her transgressions. Although the pastor got over it, Jim never forgave her until the day that he died.

As he lay dying he asked Jenni to call her, Jenni tried desperately to reach Lessie but she was out of the country on a cruise. Jim died never having a chance to make up with his sister. When Lessie learned of her brother's death, she was disconsolate. She told Jenni that even though Jim had never forgiven her, she had long ago forgiven him. [editor's note: Forgiveness is most important - don't put this off!]

Lessie had been in another disastrous relationship with a handsome, much younger man, ten years her junior, claiming to be a minister, who was not only dishonest, but sadistic. He had abused her physically and mentally, even threatened her life. He knew that she had money, and had set out to get everything he could get from her while pretending to love her. Her friends tried to warn her but to no avail, she was so in love with him she could not see straight (or so she thought).

During this courtship, he had begun robbing her slowly of not just her money, but her self esteem. In the process, he was arrested when he tried to forge her signature on several stock certificates. Someone at her bank had seen this and called her to verify whether she had authorized a name change.

Lessie had him arrested, but not before he had stolen most of her jewelry and other valuables, wrecked her car, and run up her major credit cards. He had come back to her home after he was released on bond to *"pick up his things"*, and when she refused his "romantic" advances, he became violent. She was so severely beaten, her neighbors, who had heard her screams and called the authorities, could barely recognize her when they visited her in the hospital. She had to have plastic surgery to restore her right cheek. She was advised by the county prosecutor to press charges, she did just that. He was indicted, and during that time it was discovered that he was wanted for armed robbery and felonious assault in Ohio. It took a jury two hours to find him guilty. He was convicted and imprisoned for fifteen years to life. With those events, Lessie knew she must relocate but where to relocate was the question.

Jim had been her only close sibling, she had an older half brother, Remus, she didn't really know, as a child, he had always lived with his mother, up in Connecticut. She couldn't go to her parents, as they were both in a nursing home now, and had been for a decade. Jim had to put them there when his father became so demented that he would wonder off at night wearing next to nothing, and his mother had suffered a stroke at the age of sixty-five. Empress had been in poor health for several years, and had begged Lessie to come back home but Lessie just couldn't bear to be around her father. She did not care to endure his constant disapproval of her lifestyle. She was so confused now, she knew she needed help, so she decided to relocate to the New England area, that is where most of her close friends were since they were affiliated with the university.

CHAPTER 12

Soft Voices - Speaking Loudly

Irma had always been very patient with people and sometimes she found herself in the position of a listener. People didn't want to take her advice, they wanted her just to listen, and she knew this. She often thought about Lessie. She had always liked Lessie. She knew that Lessie was unhappy with her life from the first time they met at Jim and Jenni's wedding. She wondered if Lessie would come and visit her soon, she liked Lessie. How could she remember Lessie and not her own daughter sometimes?

Her mind seemed to wander around like a spinning top, spiraling and tumbling. Her confusion was great and she still remembered Lessie ... strange, she thought. She could see Katie Weston at the back door. Katie was her therapist, coming for her weekly appointment. Why is she here? Maybe she can tell me if Lessie's coming to see me today ... memory fading away.

Learning To Love A Stranger

One day Lessie was sitting in the Campus Coffee Clatch, she met John Carlson, about fifty-five, very tall, medium build, and very handsome in a "lumberjack sort of way". They exchanged pleasant conversation over coffee, and he invited her to lunch. That was the start of what would be a wonderful friendship. They spent hours together, just walking, talking, sharing, and sometimes just saying nothing at all. John loved bowling, so they became partners on his Tuesday night bowling league. This was all new for Lessie, she had not bowled since high school. It was a very special friendship, one that was basically new to Lessie since most of all of her relationships were based on the physical.

John Carlson was very active at All Nations Christian Church near her home. He was also a religious education teacher. He invited her to church and having nothing better to do, she accepted. Lessie started attending church faithfully, every Sunday and afterwards the two of them would go to brunch at 'The Terrace', a nearby restaurant.

John had been widowed for four years. His wife had died of breast cancer, and they had one son, JJ, a TV cameraman, living in New York City. John and his son were very close and they consulted each other in almost every major decision. This impressed Lessie to see such closeness between father and son. John's eyes would light up whenever he spoke of JJ. She had not seen that between her dad and Jim. John had a widowed mother who suffered from Alzheimer and was in a Skilled Care facility in Scarsdale, New York, the town that he and his brother and sister had grown up in. They were a middle class black family, his parents were educators at the State University at Purchase, way back when few minorities were accepted there.

John had also taught at one of the small colleges there. His family was one big success story. His brother, Jared was a physician, and his sister Ethel was a registered nurse. He had met his late wife Simone, through his sister, as she was also a nurse. It all seemed so long ago.

One Sunday, as they sat in church listening to the sermon, she felt a chilly sensation and then a voice seemed to speak to her, *"It's over now, take a step … take a step … you can do it … take a step. I will carry you the rest of the way … Now!"* As she opened her eyes and her ears she heard the minister making the call to the altar.

Lessie stood up and walked boldly down to the altar, confessed her sins, repented, and accepted Christ as her personal Savior that Sunday morning, and in an instant, the depression, sadness, guilt, and fear that she had been feeling for so many

69

years were gone. She felt as light as a feather, and as she and John walked out that Sunday, she was a new woman, full of grace, full of hope and promise. She was full of His Spirit.

All of the past guilt, hate, and low esteem she had felt for herself was gone for good. She thought of Jim and his family, and how much she loved them. Her parents seemed so special to her now, and she couldn't wait to let them know. She felt like giving of herself now. She was a new woman. She thanked God for this. She felt so grateful to John for just being there when she needed someone. A few days later, when she called Jim to share this news with him and the family, he refused to talk to her and demanded she not call him again. That was the last time they spoke. Lessie still felt at peace because she loved her brother dearly, and forgave him unconditionally. John would sit with Lessie in the park and read aloud verses to her and they would share strawberries. Lessie loved strawberries.

Six months later her new friend John Carlson died suddenly of a massive heart attack. He was going to ask her to marry him over dinner that night, and was getting flowers for her at the florist when he suddenly keeled over. By the time the paramedics arrived and got him into the ambulance, he was gone. She didn't understand. She couldn't make much sense out of this. His mission was complete, this good and perfect stranger that she had met in the Campus Coffee Clatch, the one who inspired her to put worship into her life, left her as quickly as he had come into her life. They had shared so much, so much of themselves had become intertwined in such a clean and wonderful friendship. When they handed her his personal belongings, there was a beautiful card in his pocket addressed to *"Alessimae Cason Bruissarde, my new love, my friend, and hopefully after tonight ... soon to be my wife. Please say you will marry me."*

Lessie sat for a long time just holding the note and crying softly. She just didn't understand. She had great faith in God, and she knew that *He* did.

It was so difficult meeting John Carlson, Jr. for the first time. She could see John so vividly in his eyes, hear John in his voice, he even walked like John. His cologne ... it was the same as the one John used ... *"RioBrava"*... He was such a nice young man, she thought, "he would be a good match for her niece, Caron."

They spent many hours the next week just talking about John and sharing all of the short memories they had made as well as listening to the childhood stories JJ told about his dad. She needed her family now, would they ever accept her again, she pondered. She thought of Jenni.

CHAPTER 13

Finding Answers - Learning To Cope

Jenni was growing more and more confused as to how to deal with her mother, Irma whose condition was worsening daily, so Jenni began keeping a closer eye on her and making sure she kept her *journal* up to date. **One of the first things children should do when the have to assume the role as their parent's parent is to keep a journal, note the changes and differences in their personality on a weekly or monthly basis.** Her psychologist had recommended. He also recommend that all of her mother's wishes and desires be recorded in this journal as it is so much easier when the time comes to make decision if there has been some discussion and documentation of these subjects.

Jenni decided to consult with other families who were dealing with the same issues and maybe start her own support group. It was easier than she had thought it would be. People began to call and even seek her out just to talk about the things that they were so confused about in dealing with their parents and family situations.

One of the things Jenni realized was in her favor was being widowed, she was not restricted as much as couples were in sharing time with the elderly and time for themselves. She missed Jim terribly, she missed Caron and Jimmy, too. Their calls became very important to her, she ran to the phone each time it rang because she was always ecstatic at the sound of their voices.

The phone rang early Saturday morning, and thinking it was Caron she quickly answered.

It wasn't Caron, it was Lessie. They chatted for an hour and Jenni even went as far as to invite Lessie to come for a visit soon. Lessie was thrilled. She said she would be there the following week which was Thanksgiving.

It was a beautiful visit. Jenni and Lessie talked for hours over into the morning about the younger days when they were all in college, in love, and into all of the seventies things. "I can't believe we used to dress like that!" Jenni teased Lessie as they looked through all of the old photo albums of the platform shoes, big hair, and bellbottoms. They had so much fun.

They talked about Jenni and Jim's wedding, Lessie had been her maid of honor, and she had been Lessie's very pregnant matron of honor at her first wedding to Arthur Jackson Flemings, Jr. a successful lawyer in New York, and a much older man. He was forty-seven and she was twenty-four. He had divorced his wife and married Lessie, one month after it was final.

This marriage lasted two years. Lessie declares that he could put a thunderstorm to sleep. He was a workaholic and when he wasn't working he was thinking about it. They lived a very upscale life but they never did anything together other than corporate functions. Lessie would be the topic of discussion at every function, she would excuse herself, sneak into the ladies' lounge and hide out in a stall, listening to all of the remarks the ladies made about her as they "freshened" up. Everything from her style of dress, makeup, and what they imagined her love life with Authur might be. She would wait until they left then sneak out.

One night she decided to walk right out into their faces after hearing one of the wives refer to her in a derogative term. You could have bought Catherine Jensen, for a dime. Catherine was the wife of one of Arthur's junior partners. She apologized profusely for the remark, Lessie just looked her up and down, washed her hands, fluffed her hair, walked out and never even mentioned it to her husband. Catherine didn't know that, so she nearly broke her back bending to please Lessie. She knew that this would give her the leverage she needed to get those women out of her business. Unfortunately, that marriage was doomed from the start. Lessie grew tired of the life they lived and pretty soon, she decided to call it quits. Art was so hurt but Lessie never gave it a second thought. They filed for a non-contested divorce on grounds of incompatibility. He paid her a very nice lump sum of two hundred thousand dollars, which he could very easily afford, since he had been playing the stock market since before she was born.

Lessie decided to return to school for her Masters and soon found herself at the altar again six months later. Her new husband, Arnold Morrigan ll, a successful middle-aged Wall Street broker had swept her off her feet, as did husband number three, Joshua Washburn, a College Professor, and husband number four, Dennis Bruissarde, an Air Force Colonel, who had divorced Peggy, his chubby wife, of thirty years right on the brink of his retirement leaving her devastated and for all practical purposes broke. Their youngest son, Denny, who had just started his freshman year at Georgetown University, rarely came home anymore and developed a deep resentment for his parents for not working harder at keeping the marriage intact.

Denny spent one weekend with Lessie and his father, it was a nightmare. Denny got drunk, drove off in his car, lost control, hit a tree, and was paralyzed when he was thrown from his car. This literally destroyed Dennis.

He and Lessie began to have major disagreements that became irreconcilable, they divorced, and two years later he remarried Peggy and the two of them assumed care of their now paraplegic son, and had to assume care of Dennis's father, a widower, showing progressive signs of Alzheimer. Getting their family back together proved to be a challenge but, because of Peggy's faith, and willingness to reconcile, this family was given a second chance.

She sadly reflected on all of the men she had married and she realized that they could never have made her happy because she was not happy with herself. She thought of her college sweetheart, Teddy Richmond. She always thought they'd marry after college, but her father strongly disapproved of him. He felt that he was beneath their social standing, and Teddy was not exactly faithful to Lessie, he dated *many* girls, and Lessie finally discovered this for herself in the most painful way.

After such hurt, she seemed to have developed a major distrust for men in general and decided that she didn't want to hurt like that again. She vowed never to date another peer as long as she lived. Only God can cure that kind of pain. Had she been looking for a father figure? She had now for the first time in her life a peace that surpassed all understanding. She had a Comforter in her life, now.

Lessie had many talents, she had attended one of the finest schools back east, had worked briefly as one of the interior designers in the state Capital Building, and was The Design Consultant for several posh fashion houses in New York. She had also taught Fashion Design for one year at a Design Institute in New York City. Lessie was a fashion designer's dream. Her parents just knew she would take over the family business one day, but Lessie took their money instead. She was soon to find that happiness was not for sale.

CHAPTER 14

Mistrust, Fear, and Hostility

Jennie made the decision to coordinate a support group for the care givers and family members of Alzheimer patients. She wanted Lessie to be a a part of this structure, since she had the human resource background that she needed to establish an effective elder care program. By this time, Irma was becoming more and more difficult to manage, she knew she would have to have constant care. There was no escaping it any longer.

Through her recent research and workshops she had learned a lot more of what to expect, the fretting, accusations, mistrust, fear, and hostility the real Irma and the other Irmas exhibited were because of the inability to deal with what is really going on inside. These people are simply not able to cope with the loss of their ability to manage on their own, and most of them don't even realize the true depth of that statement. If she had a quarter for every time her mother had accused her of trying to *lock her up in the closet*. She would just smile and try to calm her.

As time passed, Irma was dressing backwards, sometimes wearing two skirts or her underwear over her clothes, not to mention the body odor and refusing her daily baths, something in her normal life she had made a ritual. Irma had owned stock in the soap and perfume industry buying wonderful toiletries from the Avon and Mary Kay ladies every time they rang the doorbell or threw a party. She had always smelled wonderful but now she didn't even remember those days. Once she did move in with Jenni, she would rise early and try to unlock the door to the patio to free Max, Jenni's St. Bernard that she'd gotten after

Jim's death. Jenni was becoming more and more aware of the fact that professional help would be her only recourse with Irma. Irma was a constant distraction, trying to get the car started, trying to cook, taking things apart, and worse of all her now incontinence. A couple of Jenni's chairs had to be professionally cleaned after her "accidents." These were just a few of the problems. It was sometimes difficult for her grandchildren to understand the real impact of this condition.

They only saw each other during breaks and summer, since Jimmy had chosen Oral Roberts University, instead of his dad's alma Mata. Jimmy was a very charismatic young man and was very much into the youth ministry and benevolent activities at school. He maintained a three point five average and planned to enter the Divinity School upon graduation.

Caron was studying for an MBA, not exactly sure whether to pursue a career or work on her Doctorate. Jenni would visit Caron at school and stay at Lessie's place. When they'd try to arrange a little dinner party for her to meet some gentlemen that they'd picked out for her, she was always upset with them. She would just become angry and storm out of the room. They had decided not to press the issue again. When Caron decided to get involved with someone, that would be that, (or so they thought).

A Time To Stand

Caron called Jenni just before Christmas break. Jenni was so excited that she had invited a friend to come home for the holidays. "Mom, I can't wait for you to meet Marty! Caron bubbled. She had wanted to know if it would be okay if they spent part of their break there and the rest of the time at Marty's parents home, she knew Jenni would say yes. Jenni made preparations for the season, decorating, baking, and shopping. She couldn't wait for her dear little Caron to get home. She just knew Caron was going to have some great news. It was all Jenni could do to not burst at the seams. She fluffed up both guest bedrooms with new coverlets and draperies, and all new bathroom accessories. She was on the phone daily, she and Lessie, plotting and planning.

CHAPTER 15

Teaching Diligence To Thy Children

Remember now thy Creator in the Days of thy youth, while the evil days come not. (Eccl. 12:1a)

Marty couldn't help noticing all of the beautiful angelic design porcelain plaques that adorned the long mahogany polished hallway leading to each tastefully decorated room and the neatly arranged pillows on the couch in the den, each having a handmade quilt design. Jenni had always loved needlework and had tried to interest Caron in learning this beautiful artistry, but she never seemed to be interested in anything that was domestic except her required chores. All of the pillows had little verses or small angel figures and handmade flower motifs.

Anyone could see and feel that this home was a Christian home, something Marty knew very little about. It wasn't that her parents had not been brought up in a God-fearing home, it was just that they thought it old and archaic, and it didn't fit the lifestyle that they'd now become accustomed to.

They just didn't think all of that jumping and clapping and shouting was necessary. Educated upper-middle class people simply did not do such things. What would their colleagues think, they had to consider their positions ... but her father still remembered his childhood, sitting every Sunday morning, every Tuesday, Wednesday, and Friday nights in that old drafty storefront *Pentecostal Gospel Fellowship Church* on Main Street that his father had rented to hold services.

Martin hated having to go there so much especially when all of his friends could spend their summers at the beach or just hanging out. His father ran revivals and held tent meetings until all hours of the night.

People would come by the hundreds to hear his father's message, running down to the old make shift wooden altar, that his father had built and carved himself from a big oak log. He would stand it up straight to use as a podium and then when he finished preaching he'd just turn it sideways and it would become a makeshift altar for those who would come and kneel for salvation.

Sweat running down his face and his shirt and tie dripping wet, he would lay hands on them and they would come up anointed and shouting. After the services were over, the church sisters always fed them a big meal of fried chicken, collard greens, potato salad, and chocolate layer cake. Every evening, he would load that big oak monstrosity in the trunk of the old car, and he and the family would take off. Martin whose complexion was very fair like his mother's would turn as red as a beet when they'd pull up at those tent sites and he'd have to walk past some of the kids hanging around heckling and teasing.

They'd call out "Hey preacher boy, who's sister you gonna save tonight!" His mother, Paneka, who was half Cree Indian and half white, would pull him close to her and say "It's okay son, one day you will be a success, and these thugs will still be standing on this corner." Then she'd purse her lips, force a smile as big as Kansas on her face, strut right past them, and take her seat at the front row of the tent meeting and start her tambourine melody, signaling the start of worship service. One thing people didn't seem to realize was that although this preacher looked like he was from the poor farm, he was a very shrewd man, he knew that his children needed an education, and this was his way of securing one for them.

Even back in those days, He'd sometimes make over a thousand dollars for one week of preaching, winning souls, and selling blessings in the form of handkerchiefs, oil, and laying on of hands at a very "reasonable cost."

Martin would sit on the side of the pulpit with the collection plates, and his older sister, Narvetta, would carry the big basket of blessings around to upheld hands with money in them. Even though his father made a lot of money preaching, they shopped in second hand stores for clothes, they were never allowed to live anyway but modest.

Their home was an immaculate old clapboard two story house and their car was at least ten years old. His father kept it washed and waxed every week. Sometimes late at night they had to get out and push the car just to start it.

At home they never had tv to watch, instead he would see to it that after they did their homework and chores, they read the Bible and prayed before and after dinner. He'd tell them about how he had quit school in the seventh grade to support this mother, brother, and four sisters after his dad mysteriously disappeared one night after a local clan rally. He wanted better for his children and preaching was one way to help them. Sometimes Martin and his sister would walk out of the school house and their dad would be standing next to the car waiting for them to be on their way to another tent meeting someplace out of town.

Whom He Loves, He Chases

Martin resented his dad so much because of the humiliations he had suffered on almost a daily basis, he'd vow that if he ever got a chance to go away from home, he would never live that lifestyle again. When he went away to college in Virginia, he just about kept his promise. Eventually he put his past to rest, way in the very back of his mind. That was a huge mistake.

Martin was a tall, good looking, well dressed young man and had the eye of not just a few young women on campus. In his sophomore year he met a petite young Mulatto girl from Savannah, Georgia named Sarah Crighter, a psychology major, and the illegitimate daughter of one of the richest white doctors in that area.

Her mother, Loueva, cleaned this doctor's clinic daily and being a young and pretty brown-skinned colored girl in a segregated south back in the late forties, she didn't know how to handle her employer's advances toward her. He always over paid her, was constantly sneaking her little gifts of jewelry or perfume when no one was around. She would take these things home and put them away in the cardboard suitcase that she kept under the bed.

She was only sixteen when Little Sarah Annette was born. Doctor Samuel, came to her home and delivered the baby, and he even put his name on the birth certificate, but instructed Loueva not to tell anyone. She didn't.

If Loueva's father had known the real truth, that it was the old doctor, not Mitchell, the boy down the street who had been accused, there would have been big trouble in this little county.

Dr. Samuel provided well for Sarah, even set up a hefty trust fund for her education, and left a hundred acres of farmland to Loueva in his will. Loueva married George Allen Crighter, a young teacher, and son of a minister, from South Carolina, when she turned seventeen, and he was the only father Sarah ever knew. She always wondered why she was so fair and hair so blonde, and her siblings were so dark and their hair was curly and jet black. They all looked like her parents but she did not know whom she resembled. It was not until she applied for college that she found out what was really on her birth certificate, by then her real father had died. Sarah was dumbfounded at this news. She couldn't believe it. She became embittered toward her family, refused any fellowship with them, and when she left for college she didn't come home for the next two years.

From His Father's House Into A Web

Martin and Sarah made a perfect couple. Both were bitter, selfish, and with a score to settle. They sought comfort in each other throughout their college years.

After college they got married and moved up north and for years they never contacted their families. Their first child, Craig was born three years after they were married. They literally worshiped this child in every way. They never refused him anything, and didn't tolerate anyone else refusing him.

This child was a one engine wrecking crew, and every thing he did was considered cute. If their friends couldn't accept his performances, they were not invited back. They were never invited twice either, but it did not matter. The only thing that mattered to them was their child's happiness.

When they finally decided to share him with Sarah's family, her grandmother had become quite forgetful and senile. Somehow, she managed to get out of the house and was walking Craig down the side road when a car came flying by and the water from the muddy puddles in the road splashed them from head to toe. Just as she attempted to use the bottom of her apron to wipe the mud off of Craig's face Sarah spotted them. The rancor out of Sarah's mouth that day was not a pleasant. They left Savannah the next day and Granny still had no idea of what was wrong, because she was suffering from dementia, and no one even knew.

When Craig was almost four, Martina was born. She was a very beautiful child, rarely fussed and Craig was delighted at his little sister. She was like a toy for him to play with.

They indulged their children in every way except spiritually, they had never even heard of the Ten Commandments or even the Lord's Prayer. They were headed down a dangerous road and although Martin knew he should do something about it, he did nothing so as not to offend Sarah. She was like a drug to Martin. There are few love stories that compare to what he felt for her. He was literally selling his soul to the devil for her. He went from his father's house into a dangerous web with future regrets already in the making.

Sad Seasons - Unexplained Reasons

When Craig suddenly became acutely ill at school one day while Martin was away on a buying trip, Sarah cried and actually prayed for the first time in over ten years. They had been literally living on God's grace and mercy, having given no regards to Him. Craig who was the center of their joy was about to become the nucleus of their pain. Marty would always ask them about God, but they never really took the time to discuss it with her. She always wondered why her friends and their families went to church on Sunday but her dad always went golfing or to play tennis at the club.

Her mother, would sleep in until two in the afternoon and then they would all go out to dinner. Something was missing, she didn't know what. Shortly after Craig's eleventh birthday, he was diagnosed with leukemia. Sarah and Martin were paralyzed with fear at this news. Martin silently prayed what were very compromising prayers. He knew that he was in trouble.

They didn't know where to turn, and for the first time since the children were born, he took some real time off to visit his ailing father, who was by now needing constant care and supervision because he was [suffering from advanced Alzheimer] senile and incontinent. Martin's mother had died of TB while he was in college, and Narvetta was now married to a missionary with four small children, living in Kenya.

He desperately wanted and needed his dad to pray for his son to get well. His father did pray, but only for God's will in the matter. He also prayed for that family's salvation. Martin still frustrated, took his family back home, feeling the emptiness deeper than ever. A month later he got word of his father's death. He returned home and He and Narvetta took care of the funeral and other business as quickly and quietly as possible, buried him next to their mother in a nice well-kept grave, and went back to their families and their lives.

Craig died of leukemia at the age of twelve. Little Martina was only eight at the time. They began indulging her even more, trying to ease their pain of losing Craig. Her father, Martin, became a severe workaholic, and her mother, Sarah, an alcoholic, who drank just a little too much, too early in the day. They had lots of money but very little substance in their lives. One cocktail party after the other. Always a business discussion.

Martin and Sarah now owned several properties and a popular investment firm based in New York and Washington, DC, traveled a lot on business, and afforded her every opportunity to enjoy the best of whatever she desired. Marty had plenty of the material things in life but she never felt complete, until she met Caron. It was then that it all came back to her vividly. She remembered, one of her babysitters, a very tiny young Haitian woman named Len´ae DeValle (pronounced DueVal yay), she looked like a little boy and had spent lots of intimate time with her while her parents were away on one of their lengthy business trips. She had taught Marty a lot about the Haitian culture, as well as other things, and Marty had mistaken this for real love and became very attracted to Len´ae. After Len´ae left their employ rather sudden, and returned to Haiti, Marty was so confused that she began exhibiting very inappropriate behavior trying to prove what she wasn't, and she was purely miserable.

She attended a private Girls' School in New York, and after her high school graduation, she enrolled in a preparatory in New England and entered the fall semester at Radcliff. She put her life into her studies and became a recluse ... until she met Caron.

They shared everything, they studied together, took horseback riding and fencing classes together, went skating, and they were inseparable. In their sophomore year, they moved into the sorority house and shared a room together. They tried to get all of their classes together. They loved each other.

If We Don't Stand For Something - We Fall For Anything!

Now that Caron was at home and looking around at all that was familiar, she started to remember her dad and how proud he was of her. She missed him so much and she was haunted by the thought of what he would do or say if he had been there when she introduced Marty. Would he understand? Or would he exile her to Timbuktu for rest of the century. She really felt that the latter was more his style.

They had already discussed how they would "inform" Jenni of their relationship. As soon as they heard her come in they squeezed each other's hand very tightly for reassurance. "Here goes" "Mom, this is Marty, ... Martina Crawford ... Marty, this

84

is my mom ..." Jenni was too stunned and too shocked to speak. How had she not known ... Caron had never shown any attractions to women before ... she had never said ... she had never acted like that ... Jenni was devastated to learn that Marty was a *girl? ... Marty was her ... lover?* ... They had been living together for two years.

Marty had already taken Caron home to meet her parents six months ago. *They* were surprised but very accepting, they said that if "this is what makes Marty happy," they'd rather accept *her lifestyle than lose a daughter.* Such was not the case with Jenni. Jenni had been taught that a gay lifestyle is not what God planned, Caron had been taught too; and there was no way she could or would condone such behavior.

Jenni kept staring at Marty, she was just so beautiful, had a gorgeous slim figure, nice hair, beautiful olive skin, deep dark almond shaped eyes and she was impeccably dressed and manicured, how could this be? She didn't look like the stereotypical lesbian ... she couldn't be! She looked like she had just stepped out off a fashion runway. *"They have butch haircuts and wear faded jeans and sneakers, and that ID ring!" This girl was wearing designer slacks, a french designer's sweater, and Italian loafers.*

Now Caron would have to choose between this lifestyle and her family. Jenni was determined that she would not accept this under any circumstances. Lessie agreed with Jenni, although she knew it would be damaging to their friendship. She had always been so fond of her "Auntie Les", even when her dad had disowned her. She had loved her "free spirit" attitude. Now Caron felt as if she was losing it all, and all because of her choice of a lover.

She tried talking to Jimmy, although she really never felt that Jimmy could be capable of counseling her. He had listened quietly and silently prayed for guidance in what he must say to her at the end. All he could say to her was "I will always love you as my sister. I can never approve of your gay lifestyle". She sort of expected that answer.

Two days later, she packed her bags and left with Marty to her parents a week early. All of these events and changes were taking place around Irma but Irma was oblivious to all of it. She just sat and stared day afer day, or wondered meanderingly throughout the house and backyard. Her condition had begun to progress at an even faster rate so much so that she did not even recognize Caron as her granddaughter, she called her Jenni. She kept saying how beautiful Jenni's hair was. Caron cried as she left her mother's arms. Her future was very dismal right now.

For Caron and her family, it was a very sad situation. At that particular time, Marty meant more to Caron than anyone else. What a price she'd pay. Jenni felt as if her family roots had been dug up and cast into a burning furnace, a generation evanescing right before her eyes. There had been four generations of Fosters, Dobsons, and Casons but nothing had ever hit her quite like this! She wanted to fight! She felt like screaming! Breaking something. She knew she had to be calm and bear up for her mother's sake. Someone must know what to do about all of this. *"Mom, I wish you could tell me what do!"*

She managed to put Caron in the back of her mind for now. She had to deal with her mother first and foremost. Now it was time to document and start the fight to win over this terrible entity into so many lives. With God's help, someone would one day come up with an anecdote or a preventive for this invasive insurgent known as Alzheimer.

She prayed that Jimmy would be the one to carry the family name, to keep the family heritage of strength, honor, and integrity, but most of all, she prayed for her daughter. She knew that they had tried their best to teach Caron to do the right thing. They had followed the Bible's teachings to" train a child in the way that he should go, and when he is old he will not depart from it" … Her life did change, thanks be to God. **Caron eventually distanced herself from this behavior and went on to become a successful editor-in-chief of a well known Christian Magazine, renewed her affiliation with her church, and apologized to her family for her past behavior. Irma would have been besides herself with adoration - had she understood.**

CHAPTER 16

Stories In Real Life

Jimmy was becoming the force of encouragement to his mom now. He tried to reassure his mother that what she was doing was right and the best for her mother. He was growing devoutly, as well as maturing into an outstanding young man. He had known for some time where his calling was. He was now interning as an associate minister in their church. He spent a lot of his free time at home with Irma, reading to her or just talking to her about all of the good times and the good old days when he was growing up, how much he missed his dad and his grandpa Roy. He had always enjoyed listening to Irma talk about her days back in the forties when she and Remelle were the best of friends. He would always travel back with her in his mind, wishing he could have been there to see these wonderful stories in real life. Irma once in a while would be coherent enough to remember something pleasant from the past.

Irma in her confused state, now wondered about Remelle, and why hadn't she asked her to come and visit this summer. Jimmy reminded her that Cousin Remelle was living in New York with Aaron, her youngest son. She reflected back to these times when she and Roy took their child and grandchildren back to Eastward. Being able to show them the trees under which they had sat courting. The old church still standing, although Deacon Nesbitt had passed on, someone else kept the door keys now. The church had air conditioning now and indoor toilets. She wondered about Aunt Shirlene, and that wonderful chicken and potato salad. Every time she heard that they were coming to visit, she would make a big batch of her famous tea cakes, the best in the land, and she made sure no one got her recipe.

It was not until after her death, while Remelle was clearing out her belongings that she found it. Remelle was such a terrible cook, she decided to let Irma have it, with one string attached, and that was to send her a batch every Christmas. They were not only cousins, they were the very best of friends.

Life as dear Irma could remember it had just about come full circle. She lacked the ability to hold on to what was current but her feast of the past fed many. Everyone loved her stories. It was so amazing the details and excitement in her spirit, the memory of days gone for good. How could it be a woman losing the ability to hold tight and fast to what is present around her, *like worn out elastic, you stretch it, and it does not retract any longer. But then in a flash, nothing to be said about past, present or future. She is quiet now, way off in some distant land ... somewhere. Does she dream? Does she have a vision? Is her river of life dry? When will the living waters in her flow again?"*

Jimmy still visited his other grandparents, Empress and Gordon Cason, though they didn't recognize him. Jimmy did not mind this because he recognized them. He was what every mother wants and desires in a son, he was compassionate. That was his heritage. It was going to take him far in his life as a minister, and some day as a pastor of some large congregation, and hopefully as a father of many beautiful children. He had already met a young woman, Deborah Yates, from Dallas, Texas, whom he planned to marry after he finished his internship. Deborah was the daughter of one of his professors. Ironically, her grandmother had been in a nursing facility for five years suffering from the debilitating effects of Alzheimer's disease, and Deborah was a Hospice Volunteer at the same center.

The diseases of Alzheimer and Dementia are close in resemblance but the are different in characteristics. So many times the elderly are mis-diagnosed, misunderstood, and mistreated because of these debilitating diseases. There are no cookie cutter symptoms associated with Alzheimer or Dementia.

A person who is predisposed to this terrible disease might not exhibit any symptoms for years, and then suddenly a traumatic event occurs in their lives such as: The lost of a spouse, or a child. Other trauma could be an injury from falling, a series of small strokes, or some other intense situation. The loss of one's spouse is probably the most common trigger function to launch this disease into swift progression.

Some patients seem to lose the urge to fight this battle after a few months, some hang on for many years. Some like Irma for instance, are able to keep up some activity, others fight fiercely anyone who tries to counteract their downhill slalom of deterioration.

It may appear only mental at the onset, however; as the mental starts to breakdown, the physical follows in an even faster pace. For instance, if a person can't remember to eat, they will probably starve, if they attempt to eat, and are unable to remember the simple process of swallowing, they will starve or choke to death eventually. Irma was still able to eat on her own, she was not able to prepare to eat. She sometimes became so confused when trying to have a simple snack. Before she agreed to live with Jenni she would call, and Jenni would drive the twenty miles across town just to make sure she ate properly.

Implementing A Plan

Jenni had been devoting a lot of time to her research into the causes of Alzheimer Disease when she had met Claudia Bidwell-Brown, MD. Dr. Bidwell-Brown was a renown Gerontologist at a large hospital in Washington, DC. She had lectured on Aging at the local college. Jenni was introduced to her by one of the professors, Gertrude Harris-Clayton. Mrs. Clayton's husband, Dexter, was one of her late husband's best friends and Gertrude had been a bosom buddy of Claudia, since childhood. They had always kept in close touch. She had discussed Jenni's project with her friend and she had agreed to work with Jenni to fine tune her group by assisting her in educational and human resources. She also recommended a care plan for Irma. Irma would soon have to be placed in an assisted living facility. The Claytons and the Casons were god-parents to each others' children, Gertrude was pregnant with their youngest child, Cokie, at the same time, Jenni was pregnant with Caron, giving birth within three hours of each other. Their husbands were fraternity brothers. It was ironic how complete this circle. Each had a working knowledge of the skills and resources needed to implement this program.

For the first time, Jennifer Dobbson Cason felt that she had a chance to really do something for her mother. It appeared that Irma had been predisposed to this disease based on genetic factors; what triggered it into action was the loss of Jenni's father. Irma never completed the grieving process, she imprisoned her true emotions so deeply inside that it eroded the very quality of her life from within. They are some times victimized by persons they really trust. The person assuming this role, is not always the family member. They sometime stop trusting the family member or immediate care giver first. For some unknown reason, the resentment of the *reverse* role. *Parent - child then child - parent dance* is greatly disapproved in many situations by both child and the parent, but most assuredly, by the parent. They have always been in control now the very person they controlled has to supervise (control them). It is a dreadful feeling of lost, *a twilight zone.*

Through the education, advice, and experiences, she had a working manual to refer to and the prayers of those around her to help sustain her.

The decisions that Jennifer made now came easier. Her fear of what might become of her mother was starting to diminish. She no longer feared what would become of herself one day. *"Would she herself end up like this?" She felt free now. She was in place with what was destined for her. She was at the helm and she would be okay! When the time came Irma's transition would be easier because she was now prepared for what ever adversities that would appear.*

CHAPTER 17

Implementing A Plan

Jenni had to have her mother moved to a Skilled Cared facility, however, Irma remained active for a while. It was not an easy decision that Jenni had to make. There were nay-sayers who even accused Jenni of not having enough faith to believe that her mother would be miraculously cured and be back to baking by the weekend, and then there were those who actually accused her of just tossing her mother away in an "Old Folks Home" to deteriorate and die alone. All of the factors presented a tremendous burden on Jenni. She loved and adored her mother, she was her mother's only child. She had done everything that she could possibly do for her physically and mentally. It was now taking it's toll on Jenni herself. She had lost an unhealthy sum of weight from the lack of proper rest and diet due to the long hours she had to spend giving total care to Irma. The incontinence, the physical attacks, the hostile verbal outbursts (all definitive of a demented patient). When all is said and done by relatives, friends, and know-better-you groups, a lot more is really said than done to assist in helping the person directly involved in this situation. She realized that because of her love for Irma, she had to do what was right.

Sometime we make hasty decisions and regret them later but this was not something she would regret once the plan was implemented. She also prayed to God that whatever decision she made would be in keeping with His will for their lives. This is a major decision for anyone to be forced to make. What is best for our loved ones has to be kept in perspective, and personal feelings likewise. In the end, those who did not seem to get the overall picture were given a three dimensional image of this situation as time went by. Being in a skilled care facility Irma received proper nutrition, daily hygeine care, and physical theraphy. Her physician visited her weekly and Jenni was able to join the facilities staff at the quarterly "Care-Plan Symposium. All of these things helped others to understand what it is like to care for someone you love who has faded into a different sphere, and you reach for them but they cannot respond to the feel of your touch. It is like they are sitting on a launching pad and they don't even realize that the countdown has already begun.

There are no magic bullets for this situation as Jenni well discovered. The dignity of the loved one needs to be kept as intact as possible. Even the pretty ribbons in their hair, the nice flannel nightgowns or pajamas, the flowers, books, and candy is no substitute for what is familiar to them. There is no neglect as bad as emotional. They need to be read to, sung to, told a good joke every once in a while. Jocularity is a great medicine, even though they may have little awareness of what's going on around them, (or is unable to express themselves) they still recognize a pretty smile, or a friendly gesture. Lots of photos on the walls or even cartoons on the television, music is also a soother. It is important to look Alzheimer in the face and say "Hey, I won't allow you to control a dozen[family members] lives.

In her solitude Jenni sits and watches as she writes of her mother: *"I observe her now as she carefully folds each piece of clothing. Placing each piece strategically and neatly, on the chair. I observe the look in her eyes searching for answers. Feeling, grasping, clutching. The look on her face when I ask a simple question. Is there an answer in there? Is there a question? Do you feel the heat, do you feel the cool air? What do you feel? Is there pain, a dream, are you drifting? I move closer and listen to her heart beating, the quiet breathing, her expression on her face now changes, and then I hear her say: "My soul is in anguish". She speaks no more after that but sits quietly. Pondering life? Maybe. Who Knows! She appears to be totally content for now - And then ... Her hands slowly, so soft, so steady, smooths and smooths until every wrinkle in the fabric seem to disappear. Her eyes searching, desperately as if trying to find the missing piece to this jumbo puzzle. I see a different expression now. One of relief, solitude, calmness. She nods a little. She is relaxing, and the look I see on her face is as if she is fading, fading a little more each day. There are no economic pressures here, no competition, no failures, just a motion, movement, no real grasp for reality, no longer fathoming something that once was that thing so bright, that thing that once was a vivid and blazing flame that flickers and appears to slowly fade ... away. What are you thinking my love? In her mind she speaks: My child, I wish I knew ...*

I Wish I Knew

I wish I knew, the who I have come to be,
Only God knows who I am, He and only He,
I should not fear, worry or fret,
Because I just saw the sign,
My God is still here yet abiding with me
And that gives me peace of mind.

I wish I knew, the who I have come to be,
Am I soaring like a cloud or am I lost at sea,
Everything is clear to me, sometimes -
Even though to you, at times it may appear,
That I am deserted, lost, and confused,
And in some another dimension here.
But my aim is still on my Maker,
And I still behold the beauty in His face,
The quietness that you sense around me'
Is the peaceful tranquility of His Grace.

I wish I knew, the who I have come to be,
One Day I'll get an answer;
My Lord has promised me,
And even though, you can't find me,
It seems I've slipped away,
Be not disturbed my loving child,
In His Spirit I soar each day,
I have not forsaken my charges;
That's too big a price to pay,
I just trust in Him, and let it be
Everything will be okay.

E. Bell Bruce

A note from the author:

*The time comes in the lives of many parents when they are almost totally reversed in the pattern of parental behavior. The child is now assuming all of the responsibilities of what parents assumed as they grew up. Having to supervise their getting up, washing up, going to bed routine that seemed to run like a well oiled machine when we were younger. It is fast becoming a very stressful and continuous task. The Road sign in this direction clearly reads: "**We are not comfortable giving what we used to so easily take - instructions**", Even in the best of circumstances that element of parental honor or intimidation still somehow grips us with the fear of being disrespectful if we must admonish the very person who had the vital role of shaping us into what we have become today. It is a strange and chilly feeling like searching for a candle in the dark, finding it and then having no match. We become frightened, bewildered, and there erupts a kingdom called "confusion". Perhaps the most bewildering thought is "the lost of faith". People who have exhibited great faith in God, for spiritual strength, and have been champions for reaching out to the lost and teaching the found all of a sudden cannot even remember the Lord's prayer. Just try to imagine someone kneeling by his or her bed for as long as four hours, not still praying, but now wondering "how to get back up on their feet. Later this process becomes even more bizarre, they forget why they kneeled and whatever they had meant to pray about! It is frustrating and frightening for someone suffering from Dementia or Alzheimer, unable to recall, sometimes even the most simple task. They notice their Bible laying next to their bed and when they tried to read the scriptures, could not con-*

centrate nor understand why. Moreover, it is just as difficult for loved ones trying to cope with losing this person. Long before the life of a person suffering from Alzheimer or Dementia comes to an end ... living ceases. (Ebb)

A generation of gaps and faded memories in the present era surfaces, while they sometime have the abilities to return to their youth and give you a complete treatise of the new Studebaker sedan, their father purchased, or the stock market crash and the depression of the thirties. Their grade school teachers, Sunday school teachers, childhood pals, now replace their children, grandchildren, and friends of their present generation. They remove their clothing and carefully fold each piece perfectly, placing each piece strategically where they can be easily located. They try very hard to avoid confusion, misplacement, they are fighting a losing battle of control. One can only imagine what is going on in the minds of the Alzheimer patient.

A very important point to add

The diseases of Alzheimer and Dementia are close in resemblance but they are different in characteristics. So many times the elderly are mis-diagnosed, misunderstood, and mistreated because of these debilitating diseases. There are no cookie cutter symptoms associated with Alzheimer or Dementia. People hang on for years in this terrible debilitating state, the families look on, watching, praying, wondering, caring, to no avail. After such a long time, you start to pray not for them to get well but for their passing. To watch them day after day, to witness their suffering and condition advance even more ... All you can say is "Please God, have mercy!"

About the author:

Evelyn Marie Bell Bruce, the eldest of eleven siblings, is a native of Cairo, Georgia. She has lived, worked, and traveled in many parts of the worlrd both as a military wife, career woman, and mother of two grown sons.

During her career, she devoted much of her time to volunteer work, speaking engagements, support to numerous nonprofit organizations and scholarship committees. She is actively involved as a fund raiser benefiting students of low-income families in her native hometown.

Evelyn credits her success in life to Christian upbringing, being a born-again Christian, education, and a deep faith in God.

In her spare time she enjoys reading, writing short stories, interior decorating, arts and crafts. She operates a consulting business from her home in Stone Mountain, Georgia.

Evelyn enjoys meeting people of all walks of life and is available to read or speak to groups.

To order: Please fill out this form in its entirety:

NAME: _____

ADDRESS: _____

CITY: _____

STATE: _____ ZIP: _____

Quantity _____ at $14.95 each

Total amount enclosed $_____ (cost includes shipping)

Check ( )   Money Order ( )

Mail to: Evelyn Bell Bruce
                    5020 Wind Point
                    Stone Mountain, Georgia 30088